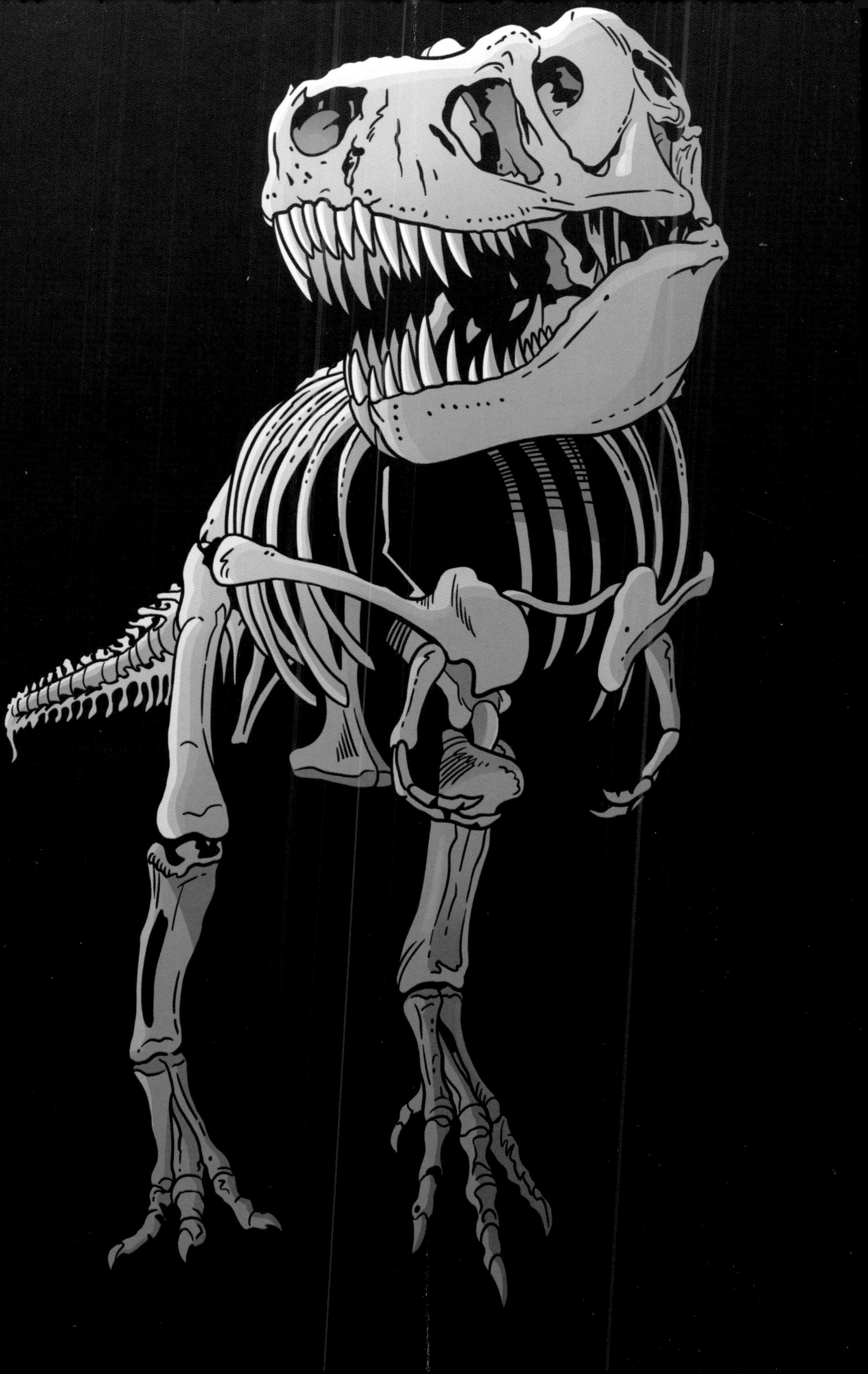

TYRANNOSAURUS REX

WRITTEN & ILLUSTRATED BY

TED RECHLIN

PRESENTED BY

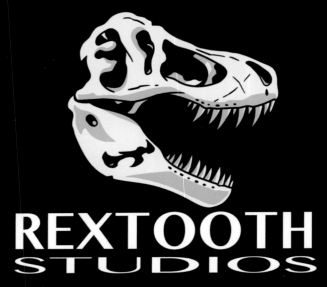

REXTOOTH STUDIOS

EDITOR

ANNE BARNHILL RECHLIN

FOR REXTOOTH STUDIOS

TED RECHLIN - PRESIDENT & CREATIVE DIRECTOR

ANNE BARNHILL RECHLIN - VICE PRESIDENT & EDITOR

PUBLISHED BY REXTOOTH STUDIOS, BOZEMAN, MONTANA

PRODUCED BY SWEETGRASS BOOKS, HELENA, MONTANA

ISBN 13: 978-1-59152-174-7

COVER DESIGN BY TED RECHLIN

PRODUCED AND PRINTED IN THE UNITED STATES OF AMERICA

20 19 18 17 16 1 2 3 4 5

FOREWORD

The greatest frustration I can think of is the fact you humans will never get to see dinosaurs in their time and place.

Sure, the science is getting better all the time. You collect better data, find better sites, model new things.

But the fact remains: you will never, ever, truly "know." ('If time machines have been invented as you read this... Please disregard.)

But here is where science gets a little help... Imagination.

Imagination is the thing that is triggered when a child lays eyes on me for the first time. It's that thing that keeps us fascinated by my kind for centuries. It's probably the reason you picked this book up.

"What could they have been like?"

Ted is part of a lineage of creators, such as Charles Knight and John Gurche, who seek to show you what we dinosaurs looked like in our lifetimes. They take in the new science, they apply their unique view of life through images, and help you see us in a new way.

I hope this book helps capture your imagination. I hope you all keep dreaming of a time before yours.

- @SUEtheTrex

twitter handle of the World's Largest T.rex, a
resident of **The Field Museum** in Chicago, IL

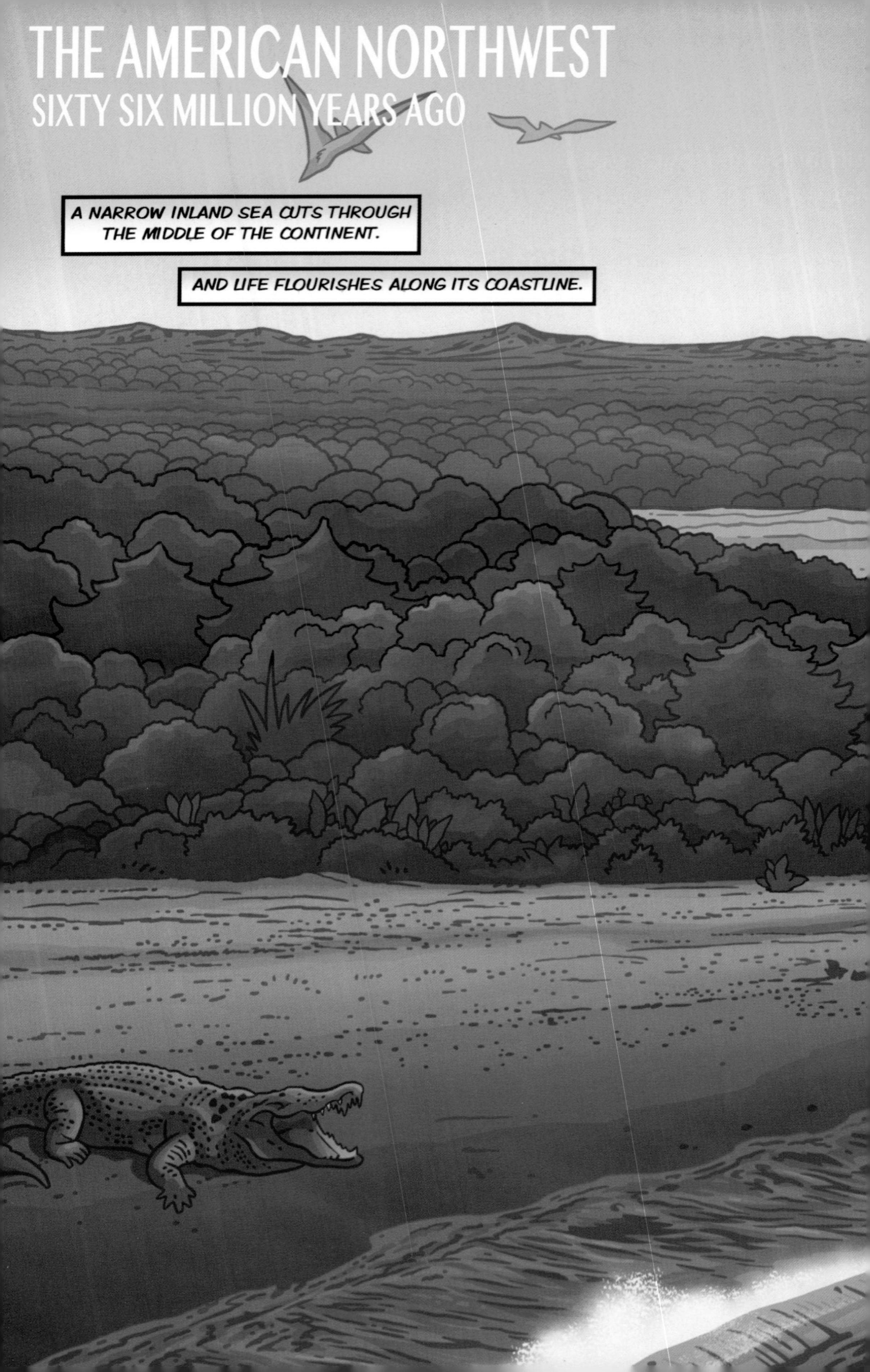
THE AMERICAN NORTHWEST
SIXTY SIX MILLION YEARS AGO
A NARROW INLAND SEA CUTS THROUGH THE MIDDLE OF THE CONTINENT.
AND LIFE FLOURISHES ALONG ITS COASTLINE.

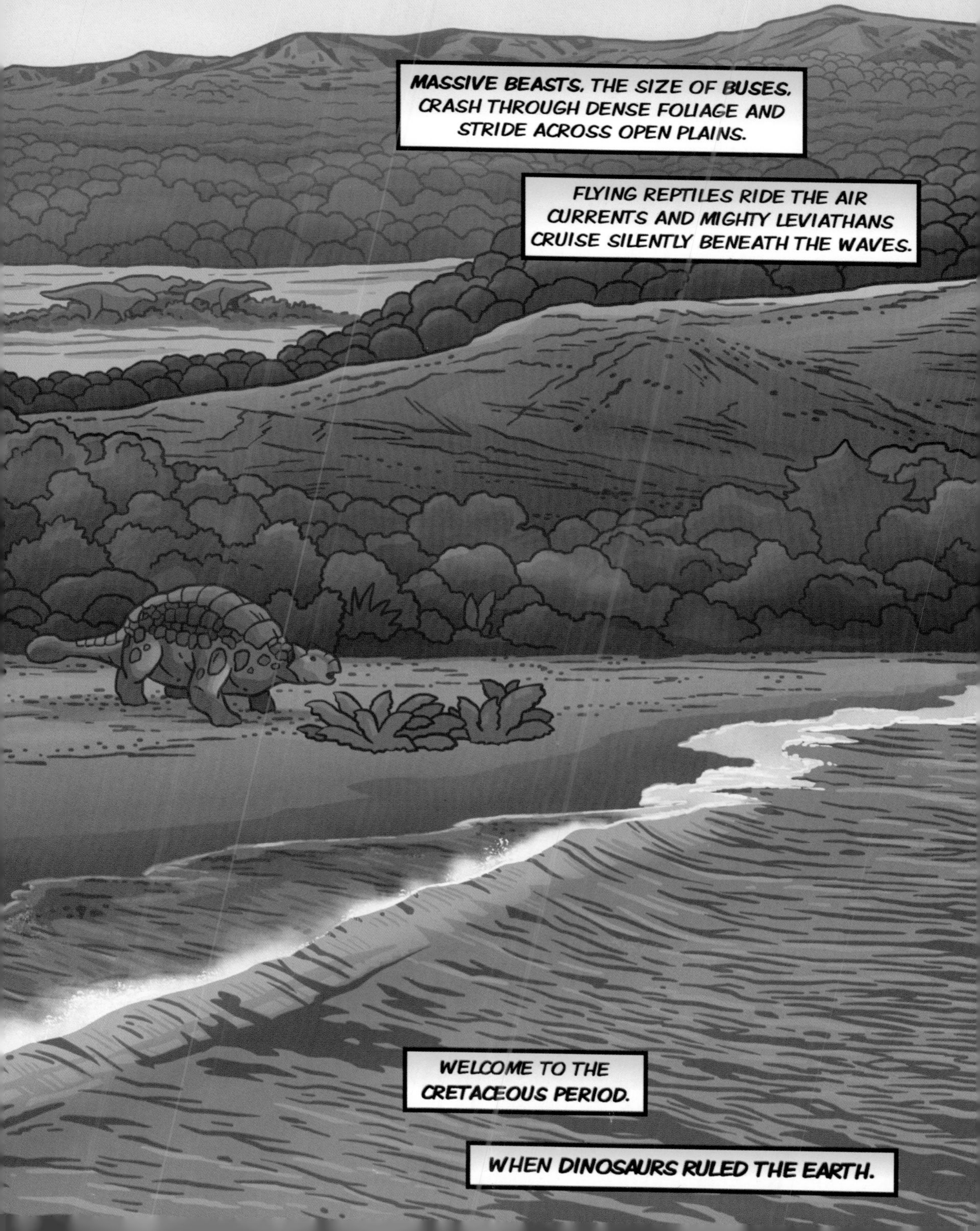
MASSIVE BEASTS, THE SIZE OF BUSES, CRASH THROUGH DENSE FOLIAGE AND STRIDE ACROSS OPEN PLAINS.
FLYING REPTILES RIDE THE AIR CURRENTS AND MIGHTY LEVIATHANS CRUISE SILENTLY BENEATH THE WAVES.
WELCOME TO THE CRETACEOUS PERIOD.
WHEN DINOSAURS RULED THE EARTH.

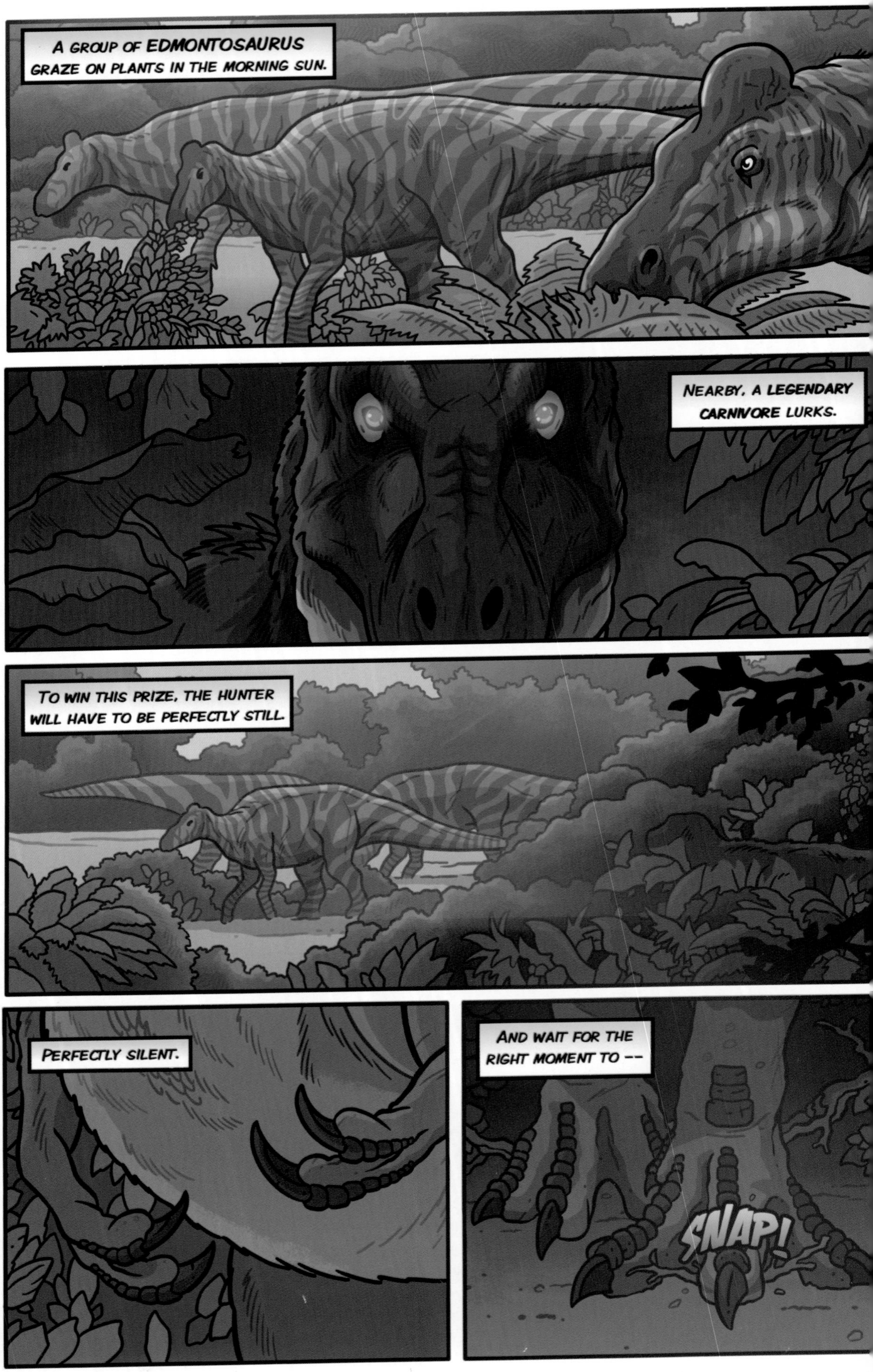
A GROUP OF EDMONTOSAURUS GRAZE ON PLANTS IN THE MORNING SUN.
NEARBY, A LEGENDARY CARNIVORE LURKS.
TO WIN THIS PRIZE, THE HUNTER WILL HAVE TO BE PERFECTLY STILL.
PERFECTLY SILENT.
AND WAIT FOR THE RIGHT MOMENT TO --
SNAP!

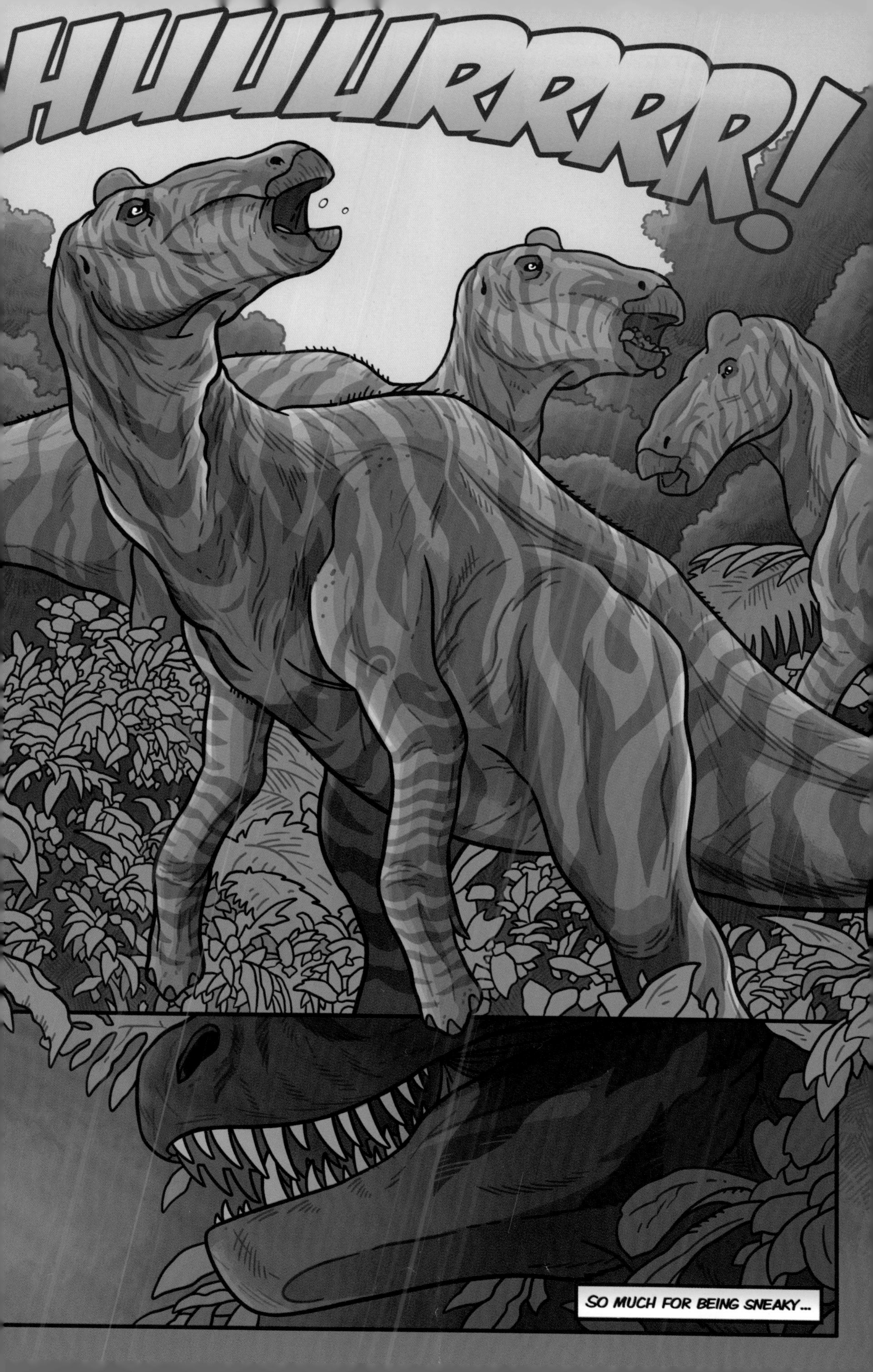
HUUURRRRR!
SO MUCH FOR BEING SNEAKY...

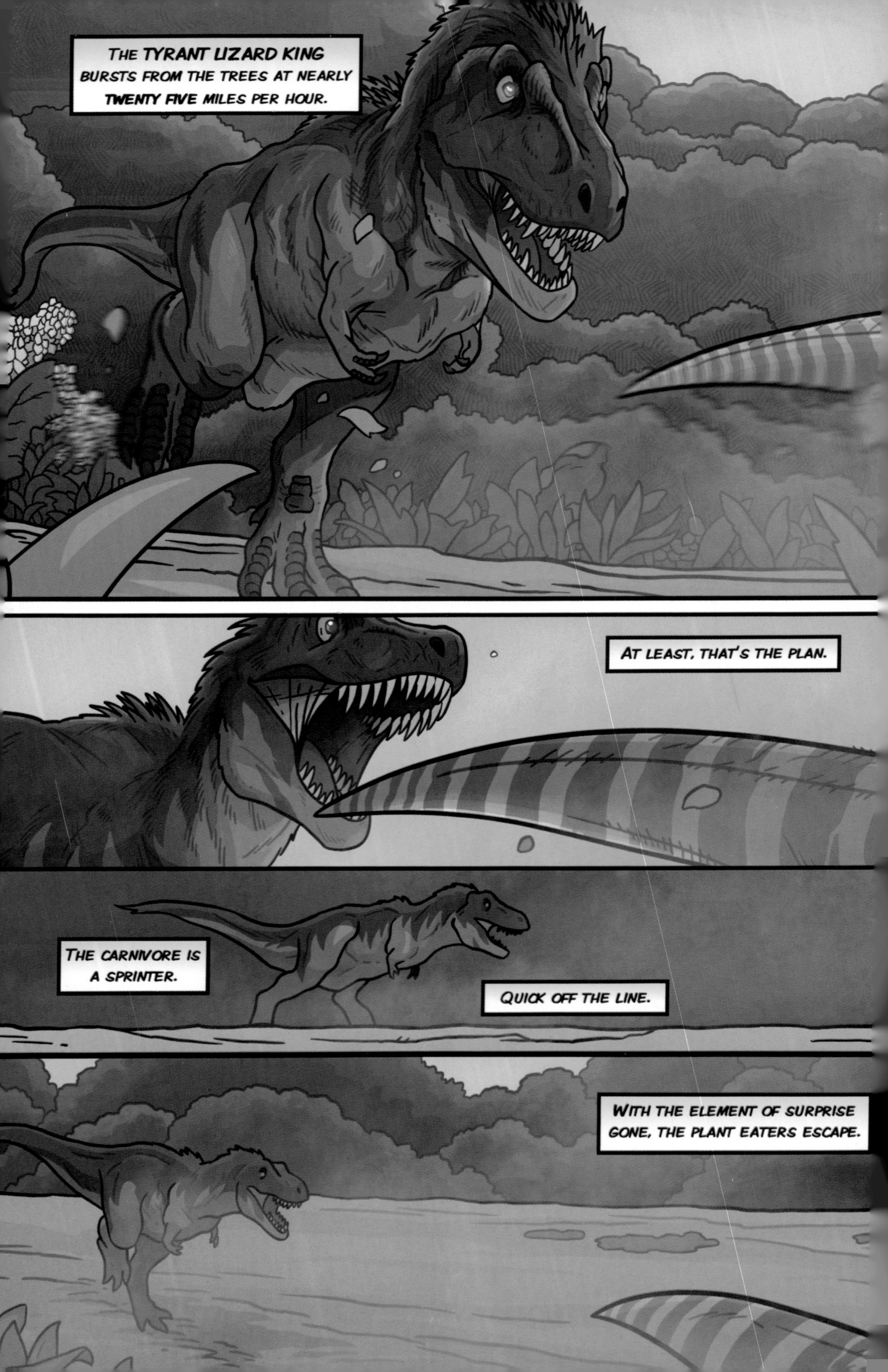
THE TYRANT LIZARD KING BURSTS FROM THE TREES AT NEARLY TWENTY FIVE MILES PER HOUR.
AT LEAST, THAT'S THE PLAN.
THE CARNIVORE IS A SPRINTER.
QUICK OFF THE LINE.
WITH THE ELEMENT OF SURPRISE GONE, THE PLANT EATERS ESCAPE.

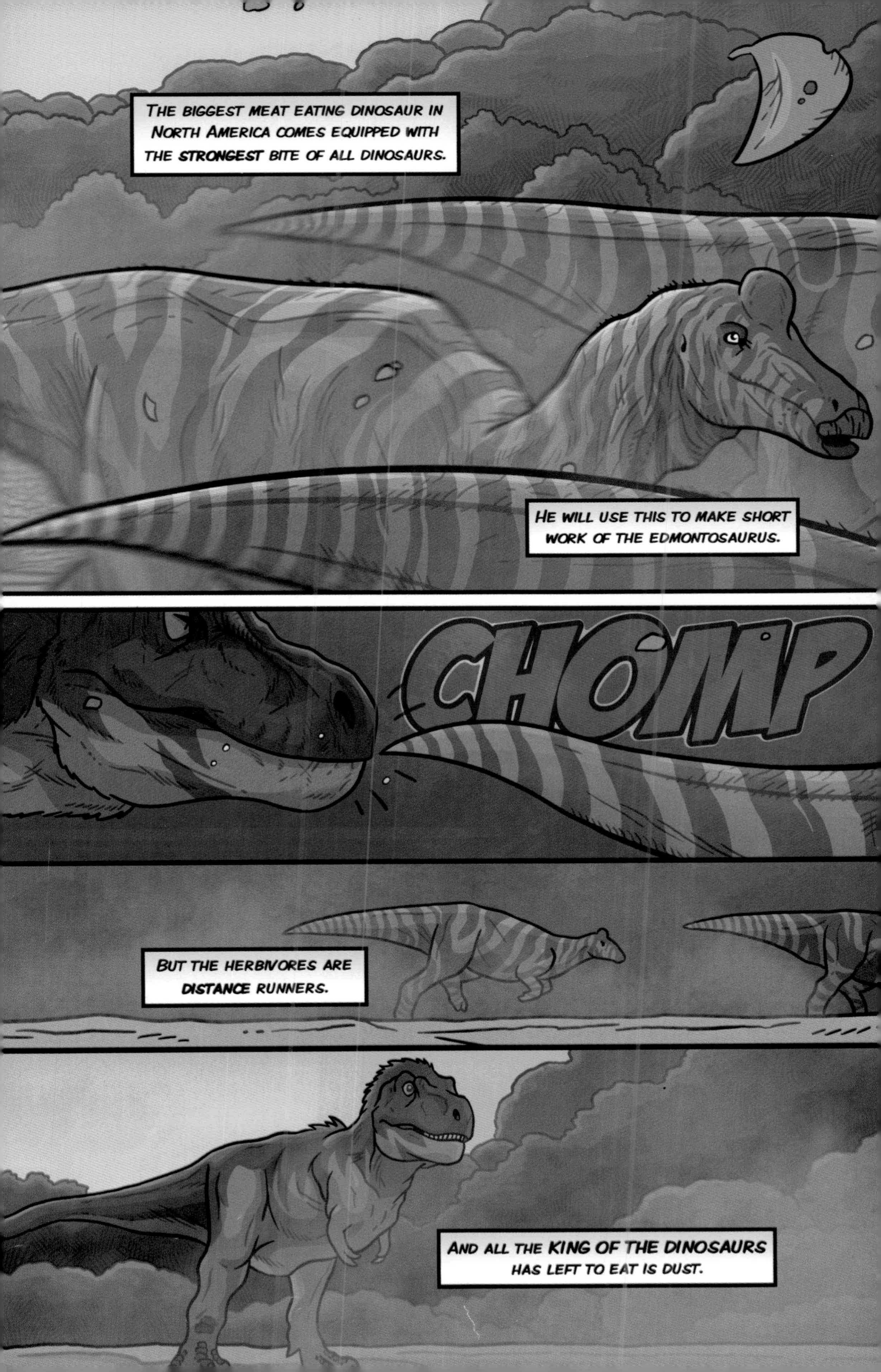
THE BIGGEST MEAT EATING DINOSAUR IN NORTH AMERICA COMES EQUIPPED WITH THE STRONGEST BITE OF ALL DINOSAURS.
HE WILL USE THIS TO MAKE SHORT WORK OF THE EDMONTOSAURUS.
CHOMP
BUT THE HERBIVORES ARE DISTANCE RUNNERS.
AND ALL THE KING OF THE DINOSAURS HAS LEFT TO EAT IS DUST.

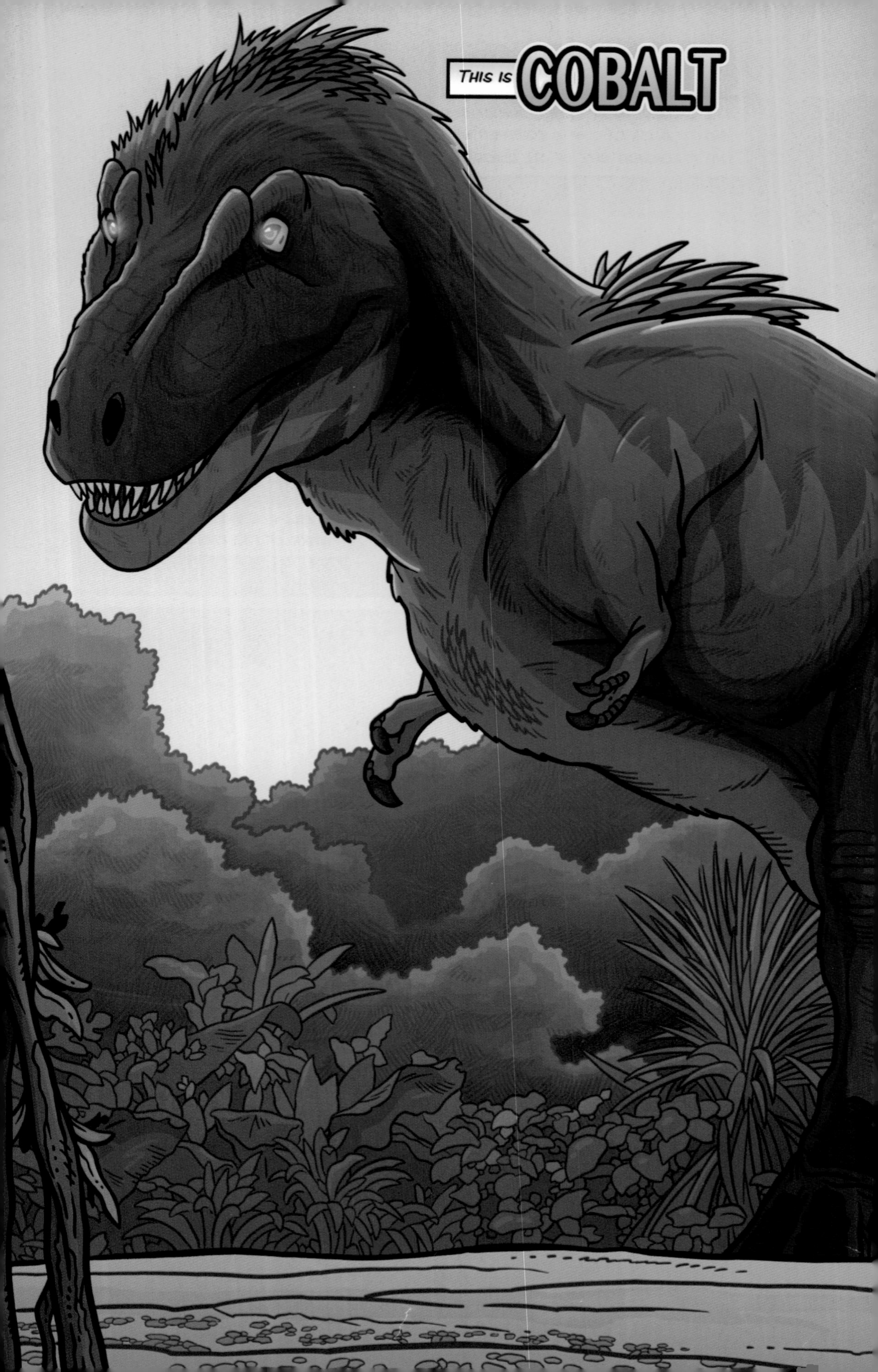
THIS IS COBALT

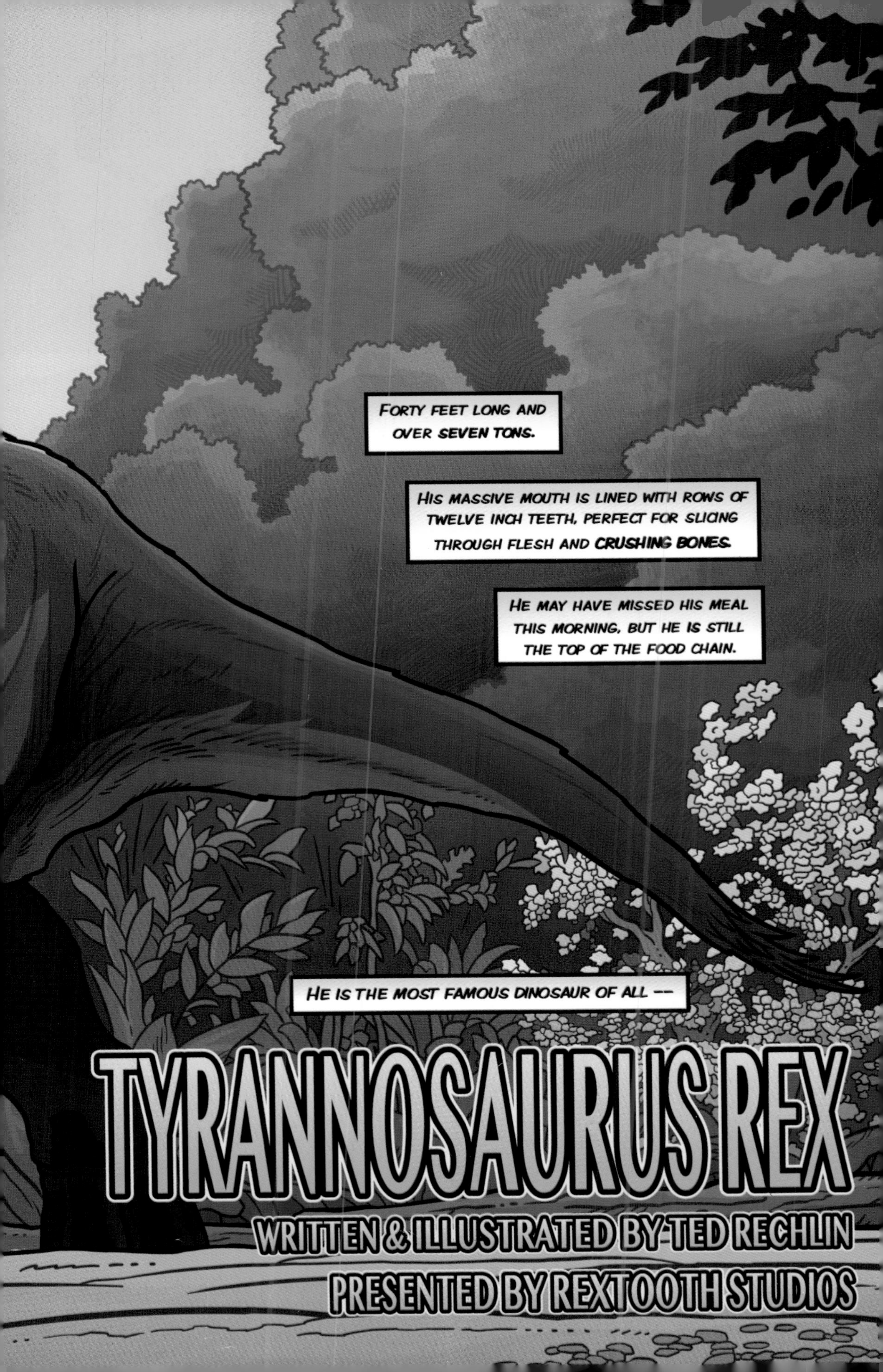
FORTY FEET LONG AND OVER SEVEN TONS.
HIS MASSIVE MOUTH IS LINED WITH ROWS OF TWELVE INCH TEETH, PERFECT FOR SLICING THROUGH FLESH AND CRUSHING BONES.
HE MAY HAVE MISSED HIS MEAL THIS MORNING, BUT HE IS STILL THE TOP OF THE FOOD CHAIN.
HE IS THE MOST FAMOUS DINOSAUR OF ALL --
TYRANNOSAURUS REX
WRITTEN & ILLUSTRATED BY TED RECHLIN
PRESENTED BY REXTOOTH STUDIOS

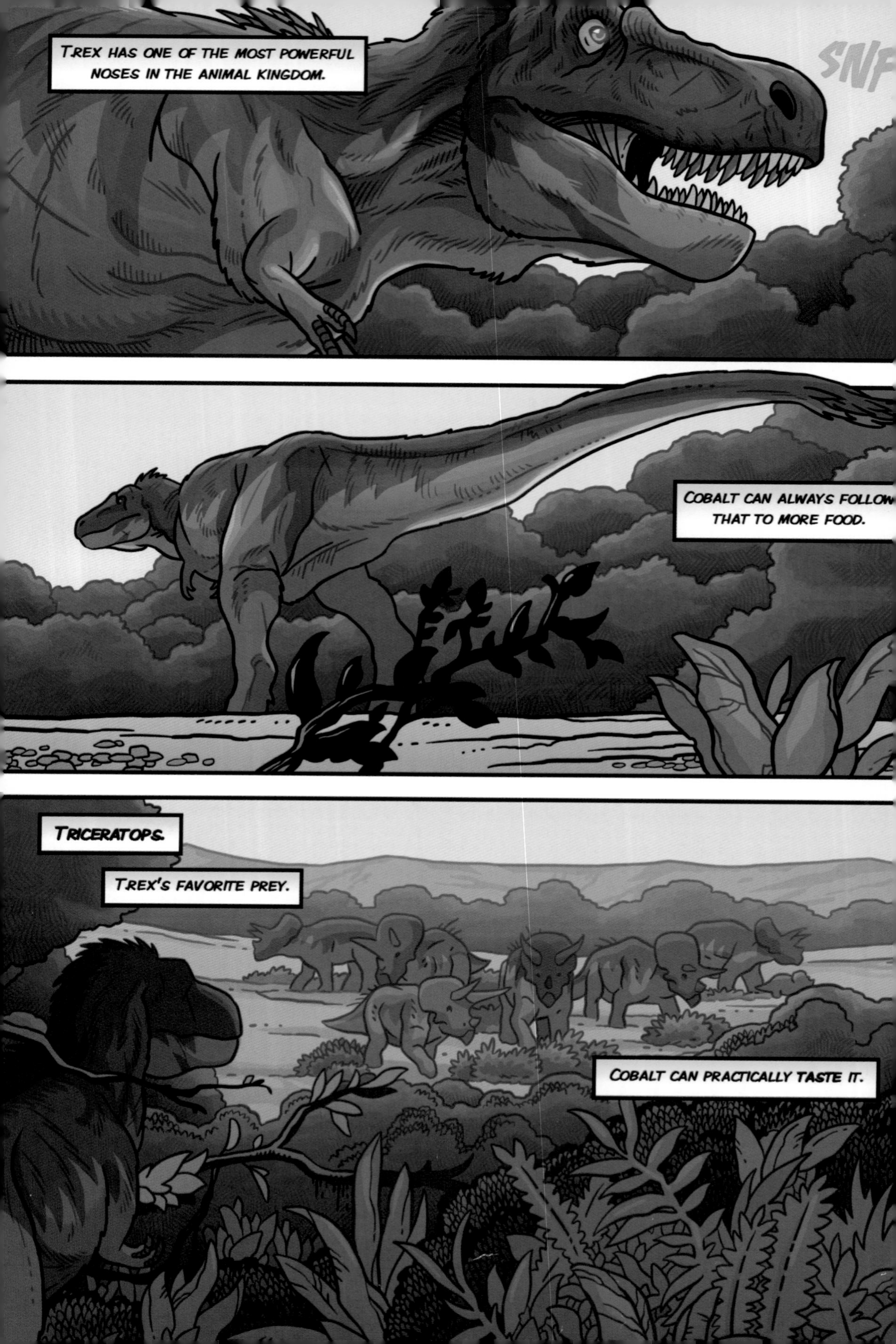
T.REX HAS ONE OF THE MOST POWERFUL NOSES IN THE ANIMAL KINGDOM.
SNF
COBALT CAN ALWAYS FOLLOW THAT TO MORE FOOD.
TRICERATOPS.
T.REX'S FAVORITE PREY.
COBALT CAN PRACTICALLY TASTE IT.

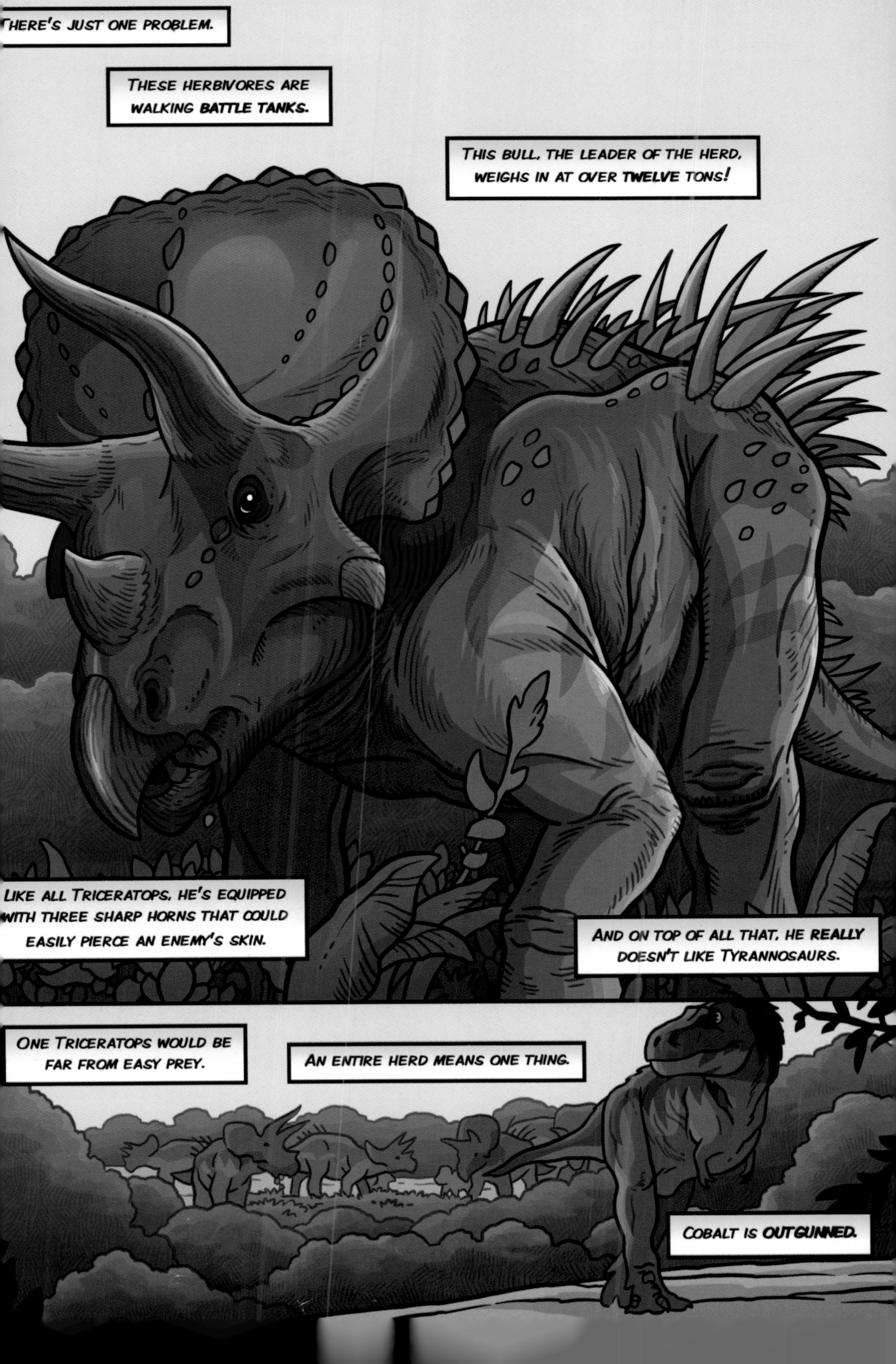
THERE'S JUST ONE PROBLEM.
THESE HERBIVORES ARE WALKING BATTLE TANKS.
THIS BULL, THE LEADER OF THE HERD, WEIGHS IN AT OVER TWELVE TONS!
LIKE ALL TRICERATOPS, HE'S EQUIPPED WITH THREE SHARP HORNS THAT COULD EASILY PIERCE AN ENEMY'S SKIN.
AND ON TOP OF ALL THAT, HE REALLY DOESN'T LIKE TYRANNOSAURS.
ONE TRICERATOPS WOULD BE FAR FROM EASY PREY.
AN ENTIRE HERD MEANS ONE THING.
COBALT IS OUTGUNNED.

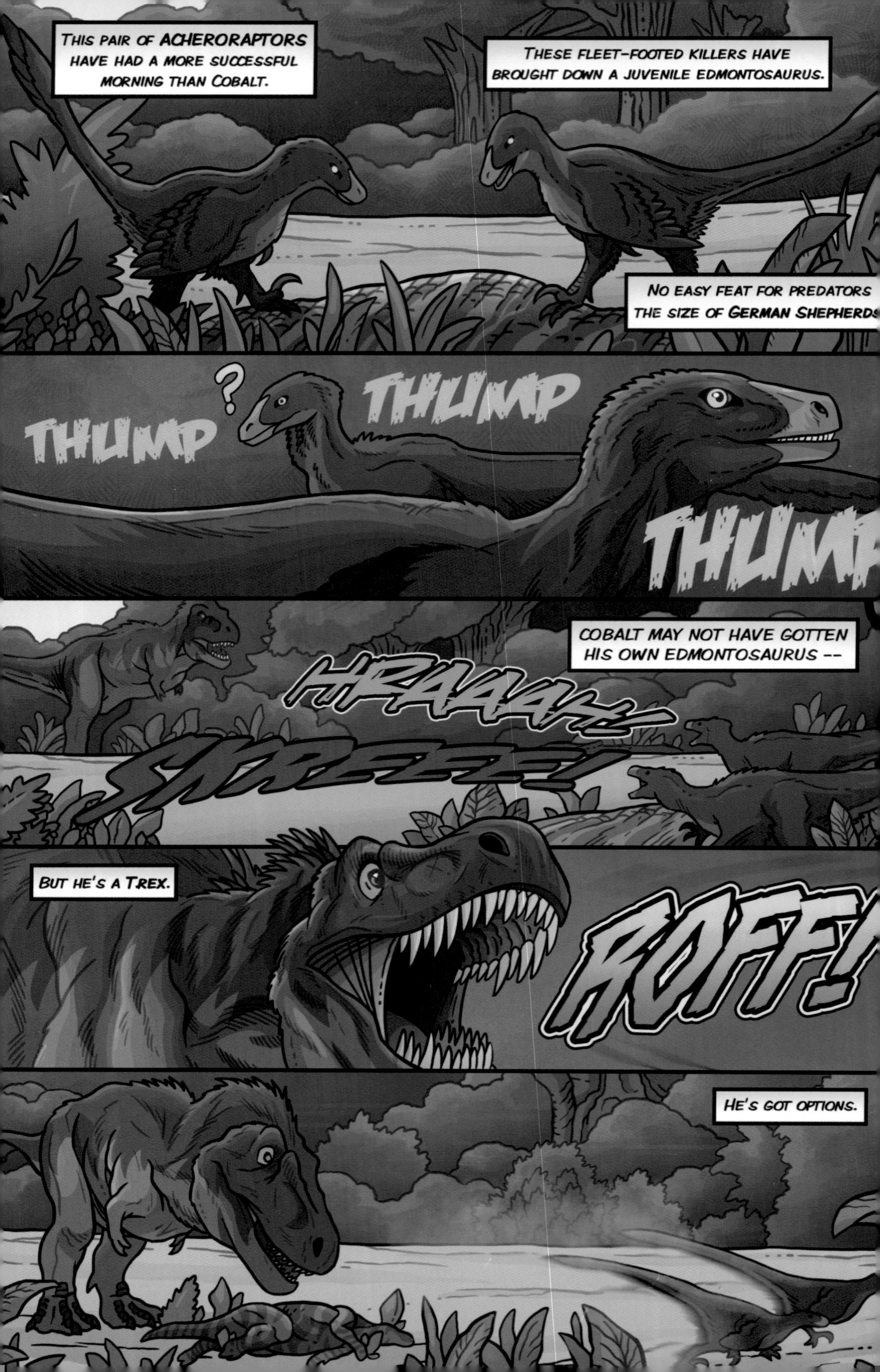
THIS PAIR OF ACHERORAPTORS HAVE HAD A MORE SUCCESSFUL MORNING THAN COBALT.
THESE FLEET-FOOTED KILLERS HAVE BROUGHT DOWN A JUVENILE EDMONTOSAURUS.
NO EASY FEAT FOR PREDATORS THE SIZE OF GERMAN SHEPHERDS
THUMP
?
THUMP
THUMP
COBALT MAY NOT HAVE GOTTEN HIS OWN EDMONTOSAURUS --
HRAAAK!
SKREEEE!
BUT HE'S A T.REX.
ROFF!
HE'S GOT OPTIONS.

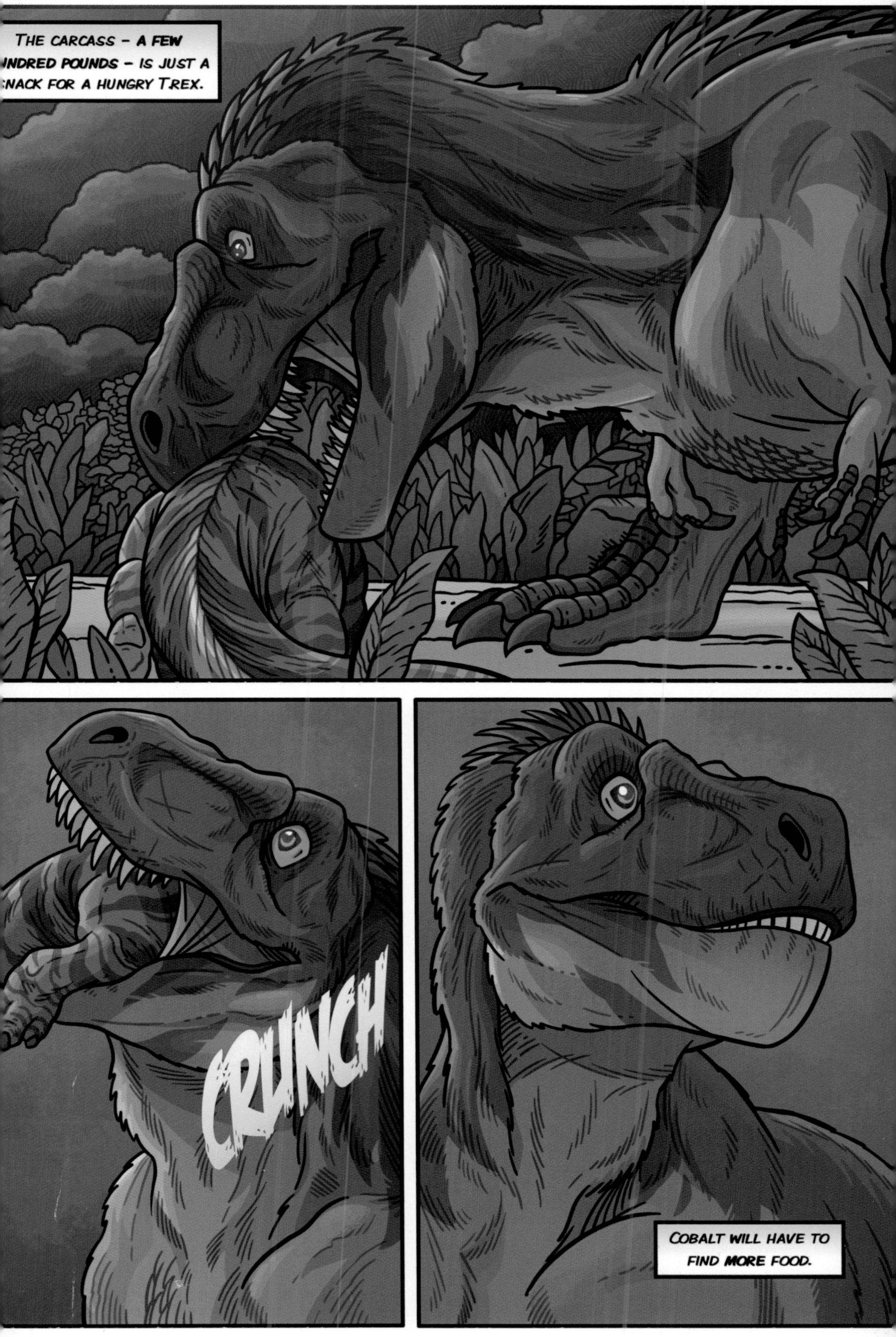
THE CARCASS - A FEW
HUNDRED POUNDS - IS JUST A
SNACK FOR A HUNGRY T.REX.
CRUNCH
COBALT WILL HAVE TO
FIND MORE FOOD.

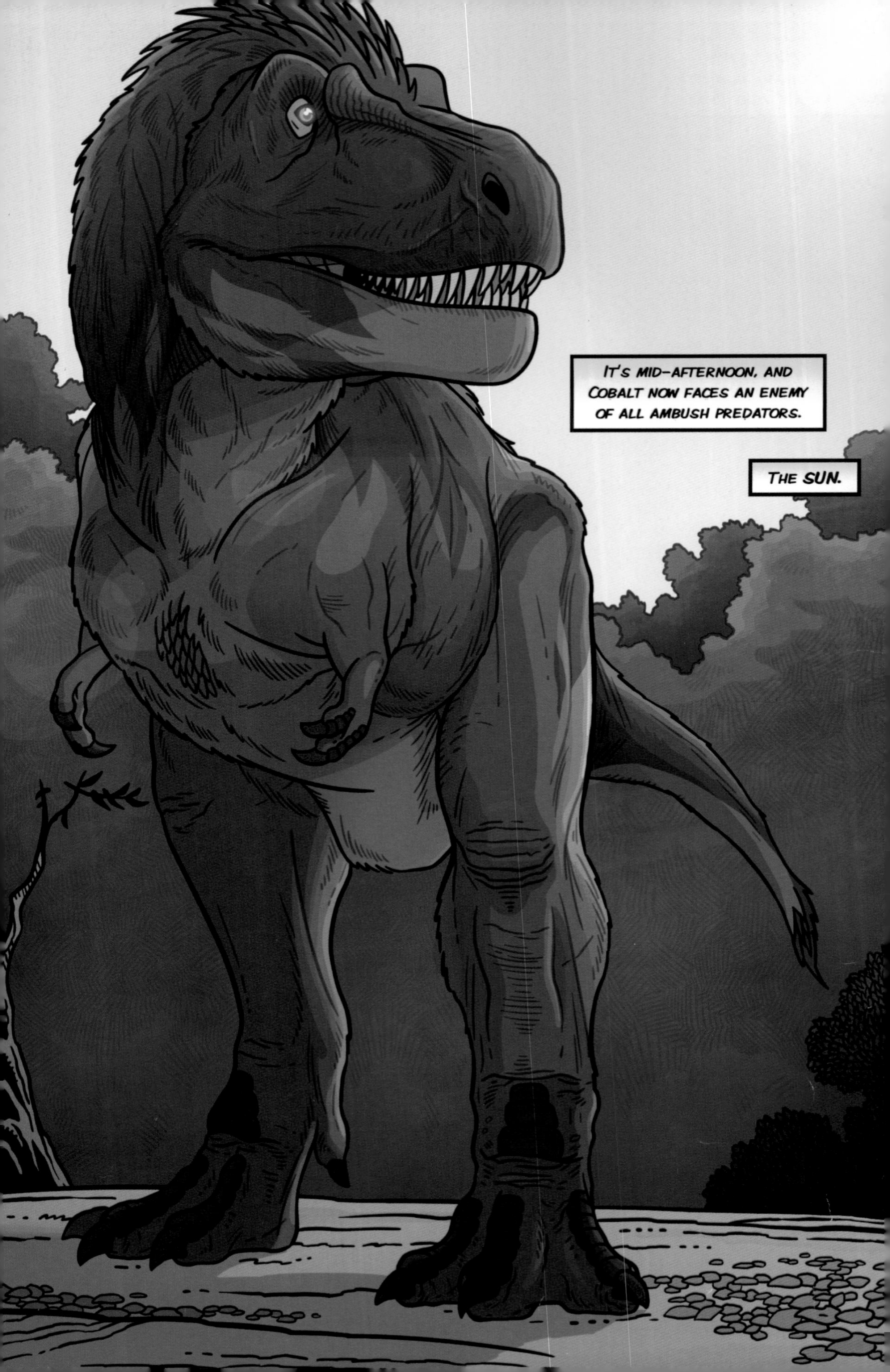
IT'S MID-AFTERNOON, AND COBALT NOW FACES AN ENEMY OF ALL AMBUSH PREDATORS.
THE SUN.

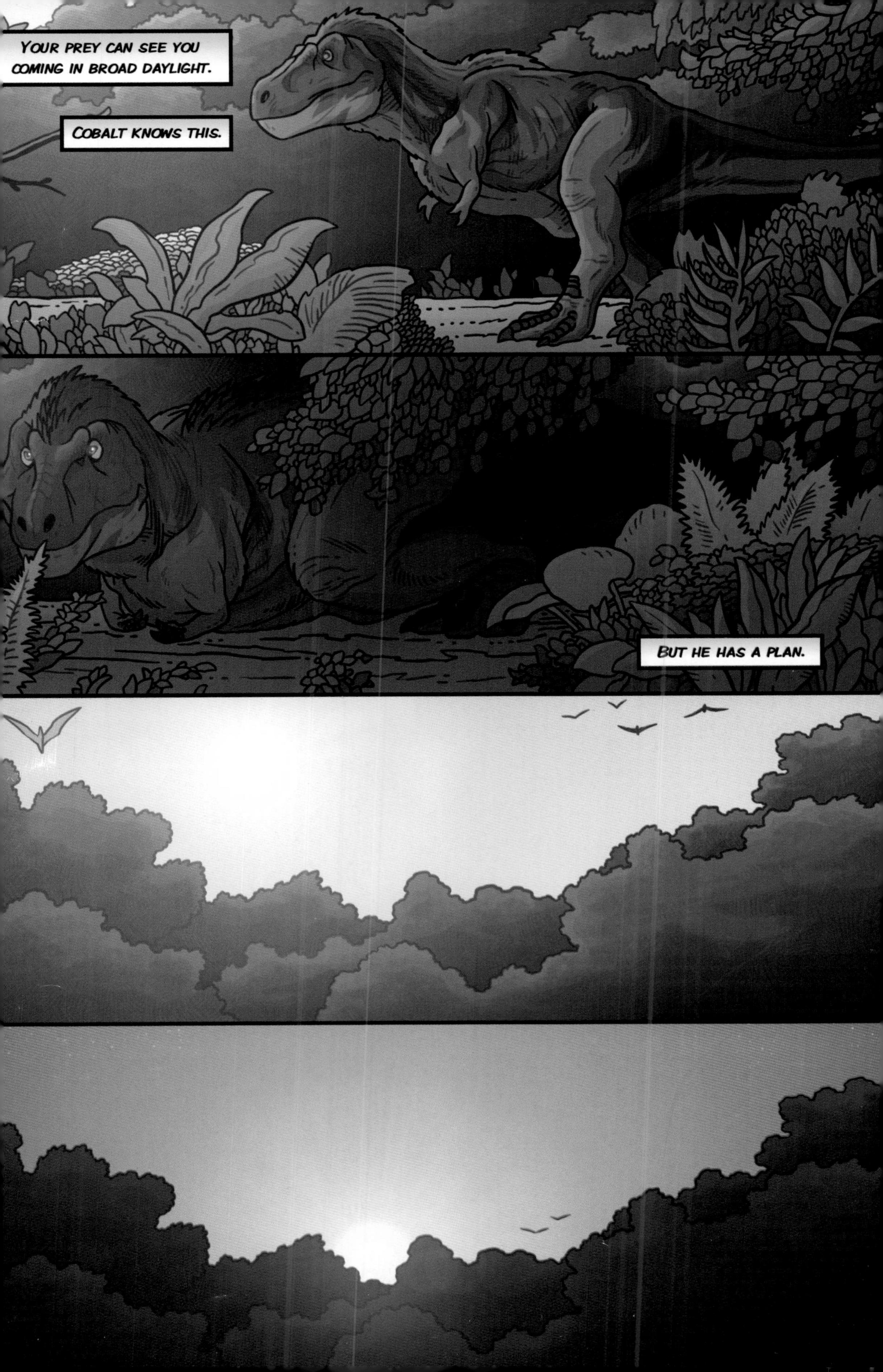
YOUR PREY CAN SEE YOU COMING IN BROAD DAYLIGHT.
COBALT KNOWS THIS.
BUT HE HAS A PLAN.

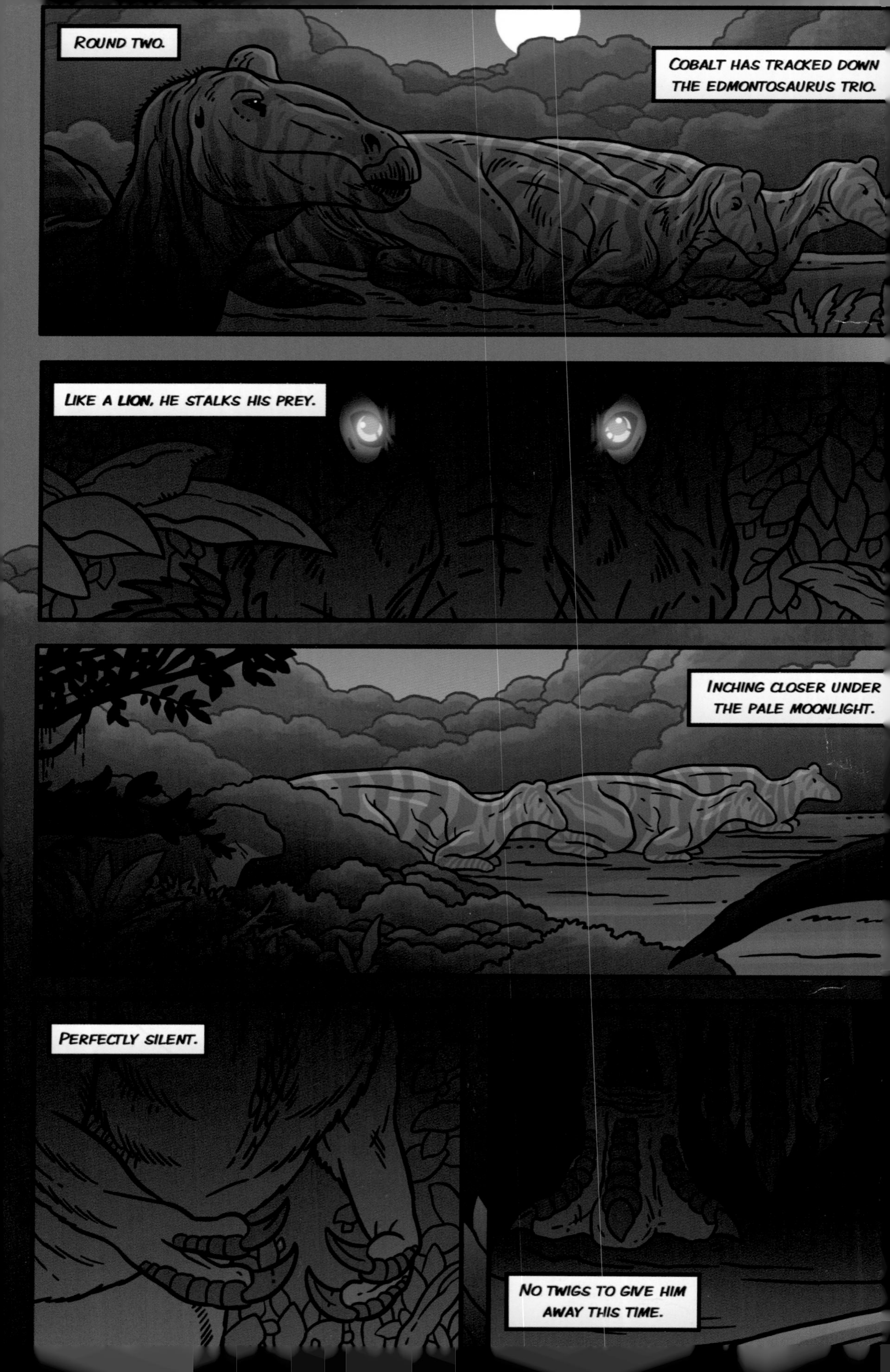
ROUND TWO.
COBALT HAS TRACKED DOWN THE EDMONTOSAURUS TRIO.
LIKE A **LION**, HE STALKS HIS PREY.
INCHING CLOSER UNDER THE PALE MOONLIGHT.
PERFECTLY SILENT.
NO TWIGS TO GIVE HIM AWAY THIS TIME.

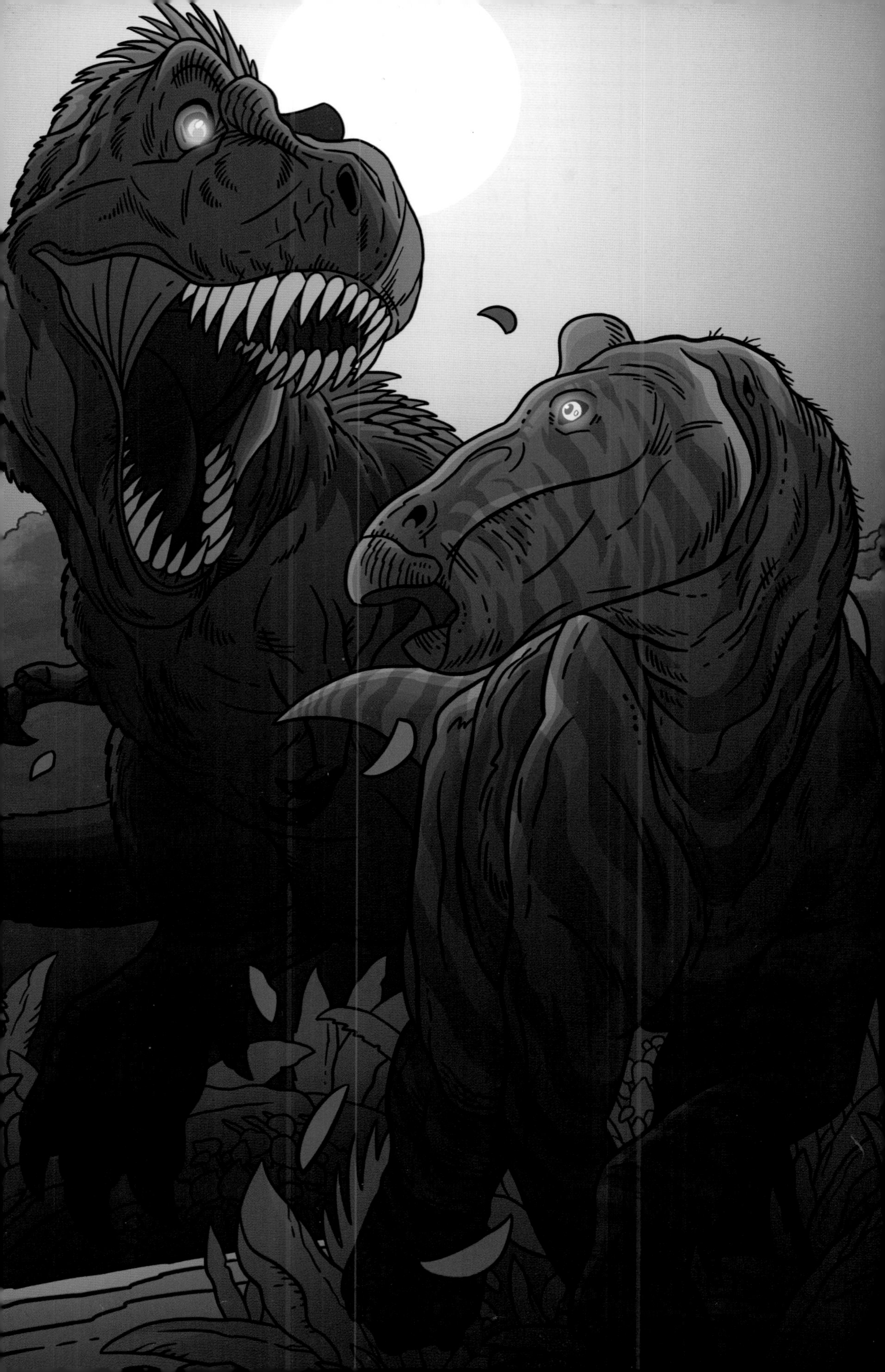

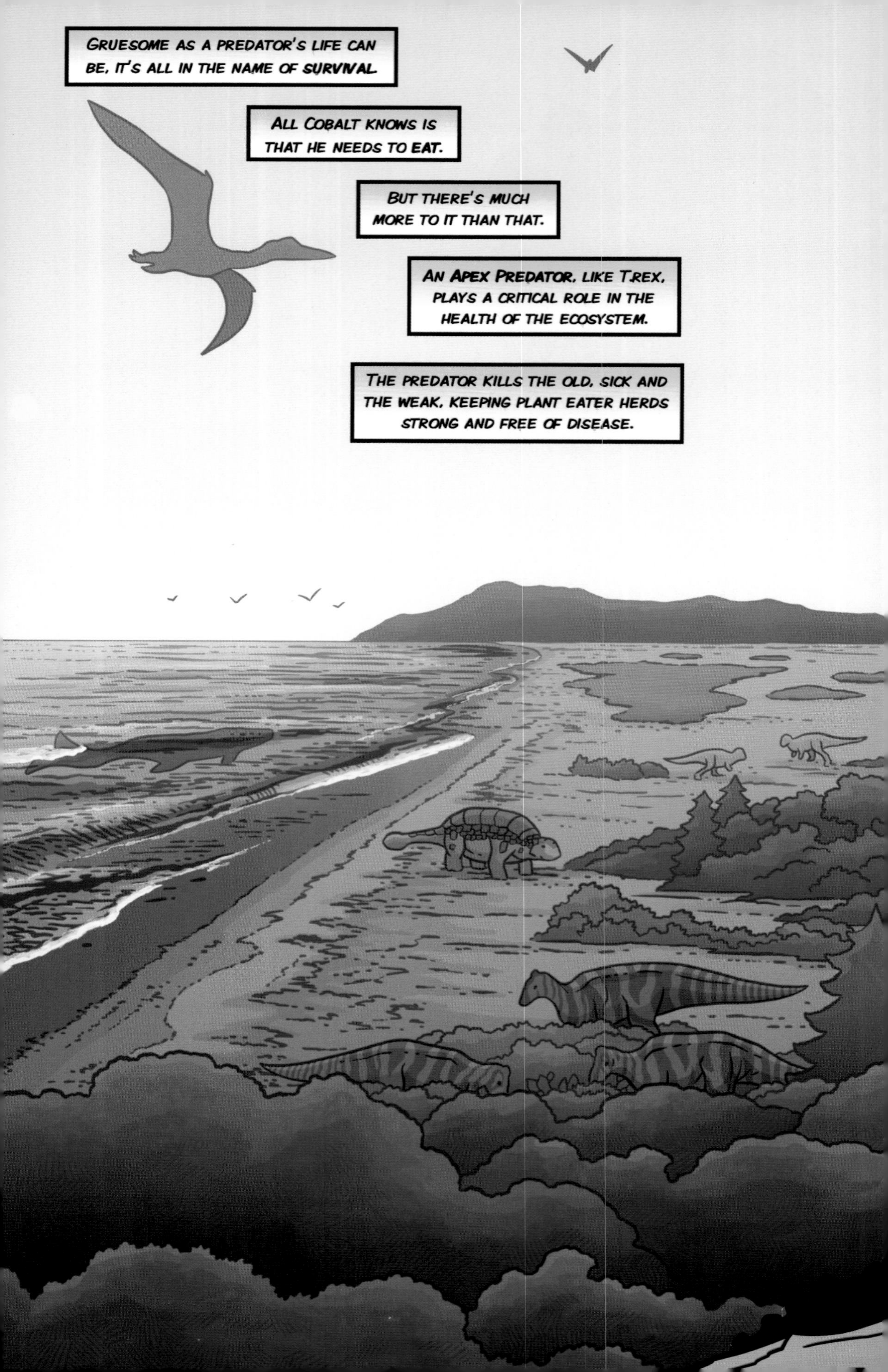
GRUESOME AS A PREDATOR'S LIFE CAN BE, IT'S ALL IN THE NAME OF SURVIVAL
ALL COBALT KNOWS IS THAT HE NEEDS TO EAT.
BUT THERE'S MUCH MORE TO IT THAN THAT.
AN APEX PREDATOR, LIKE T.REX, PLAYS A CRITICAL ROLE IN THE HEALTH OF THE ECOSYSTEM.
THE PREDATOR KILLS THE OLD, SICK AND THE WEAK, KEEPING PLANT EATER HERDS STRONG AND FREE OF DISEASE.

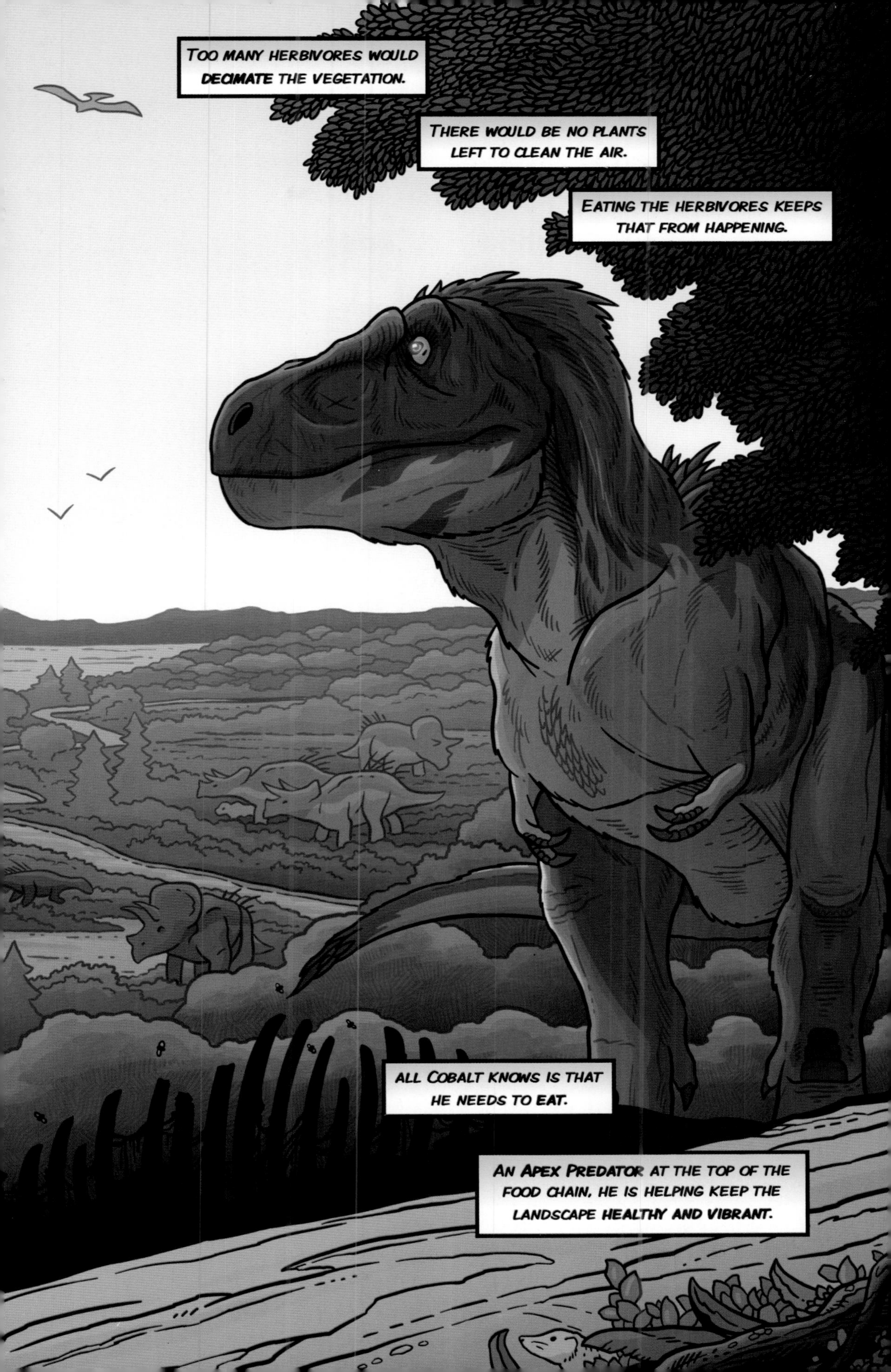
Too many herbivores would decimate the vegetation.
There would be no plants left to clean the air.
Eating the herbivores keeps that from happening.
All Cobalt knows is that he needs to eat.
An Apex Predator at the top of the food chain, he is helping keep the landscape healthy and vibrant.

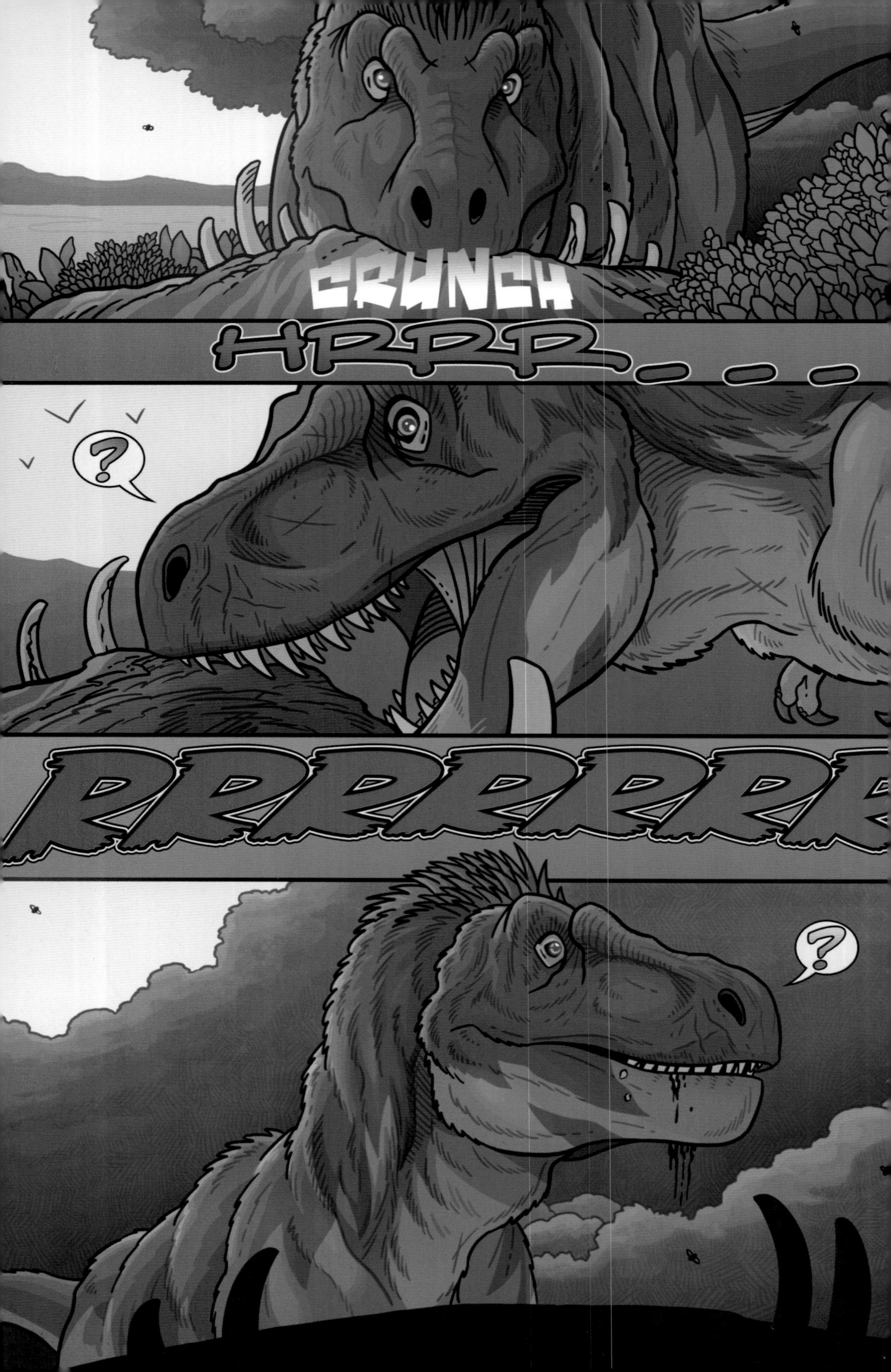
CRUNCH
HRRR...
?
RRRRRRR
?

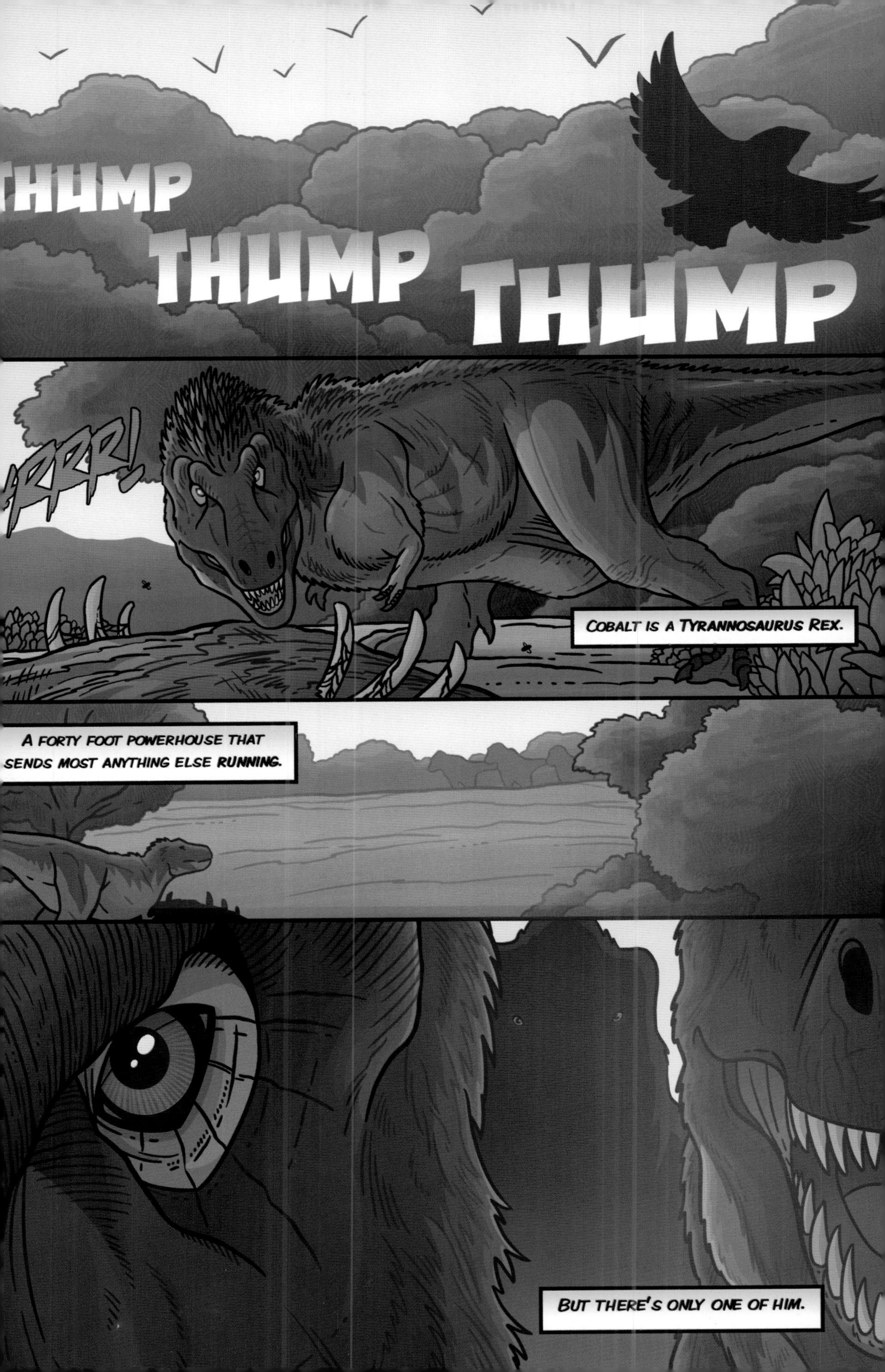
THUMP
THUMP
THUMP
COBALT IS A TYRANNOSAURUS REX.
A FORTY FOOT POWERHOUSE THAT SENDS MOST ANYTHING ELSE RUNNING.
BUT THERE'S ONLY ONE OF HIM.

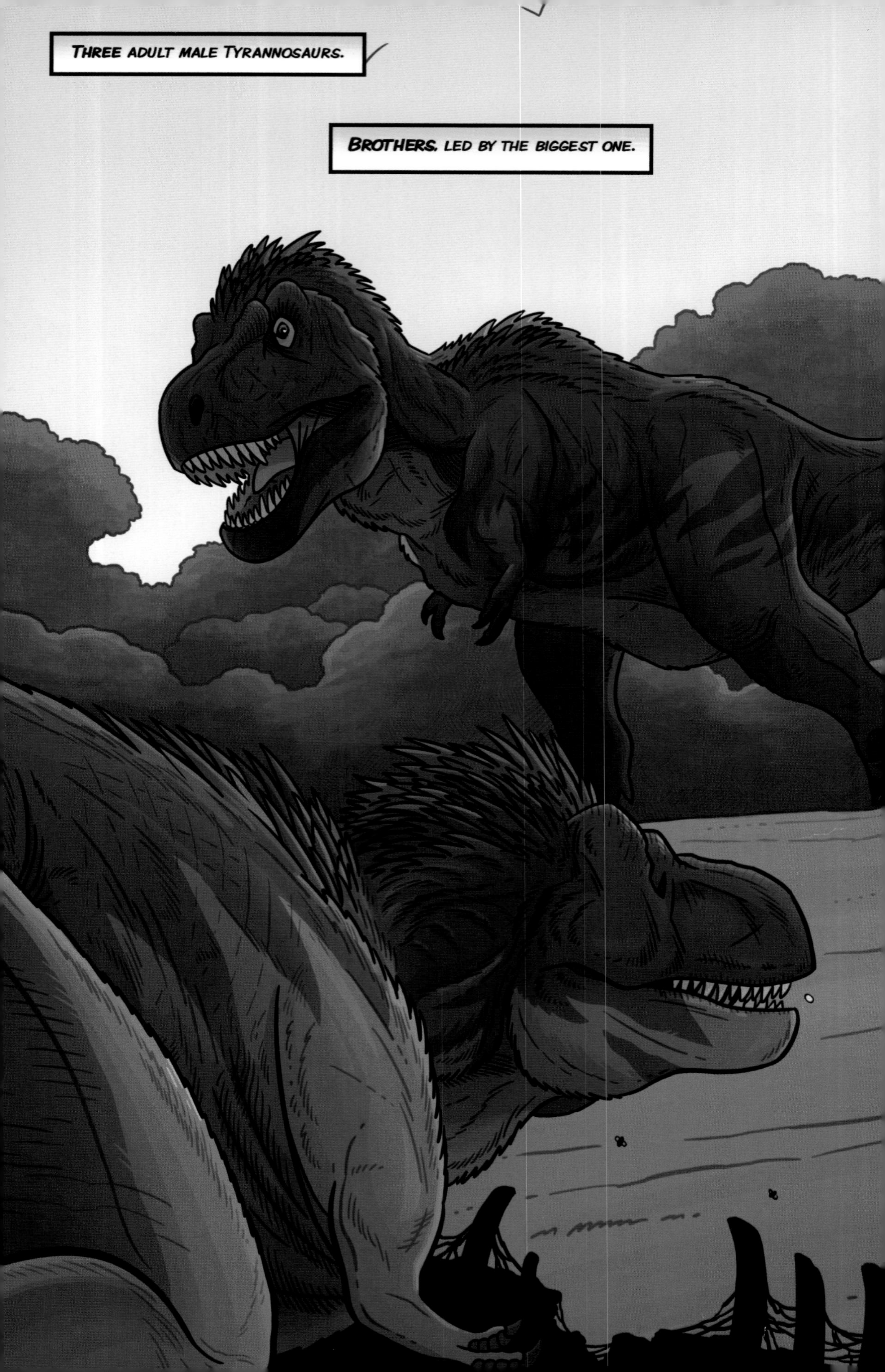
THREE ADULT MALE TYRANNOSAURS.
BROTHERS, LED BY THE BIGGEST ONE.

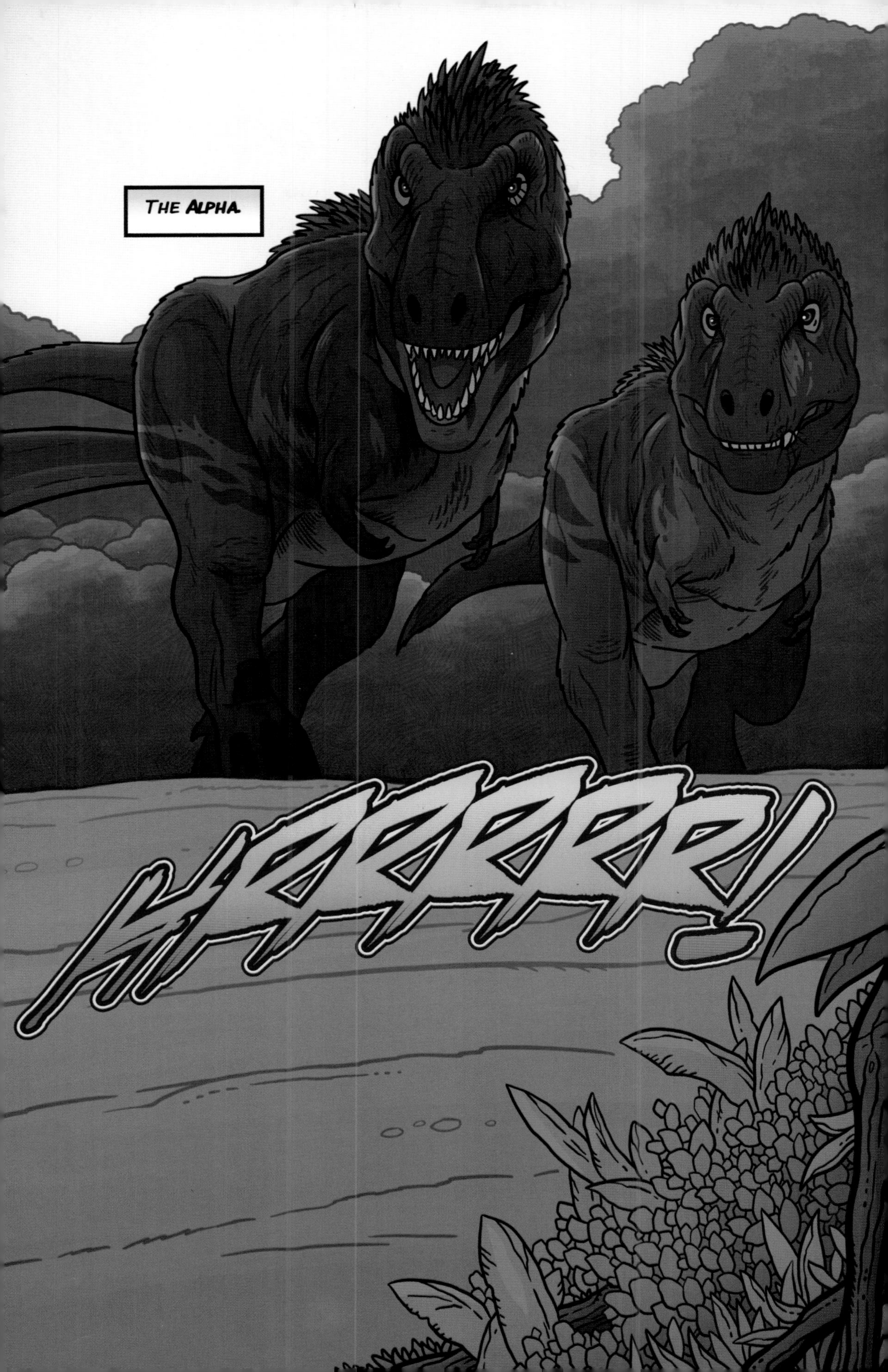
THE ALPHA
HRRRRR!

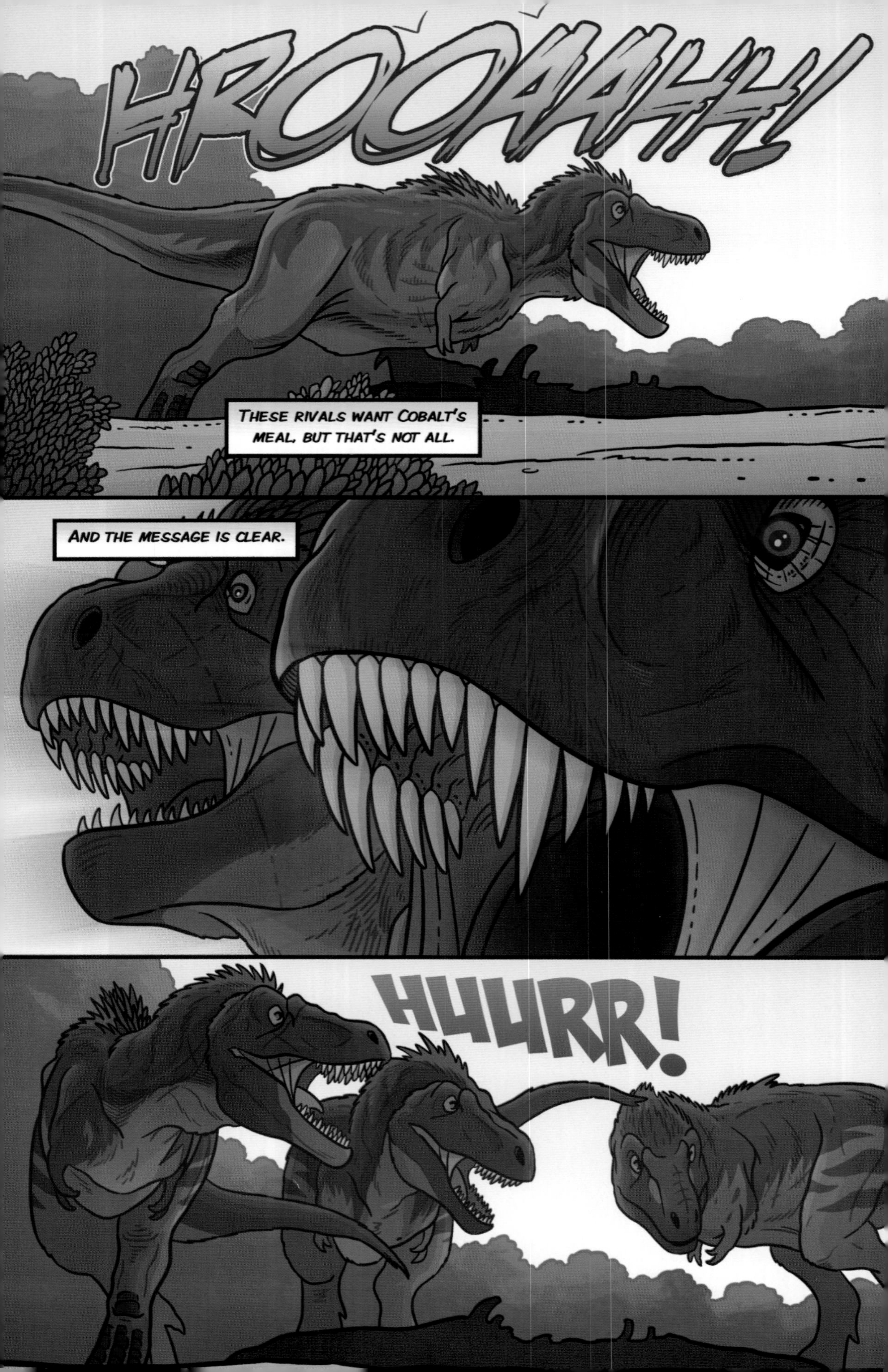
HROOAAHH!
THESE RIVALS WANT COBALT'S MEAL, BUT THAT'S NOT ALL.
AND THE MESSAGE IS CLEAR.
HUURR!

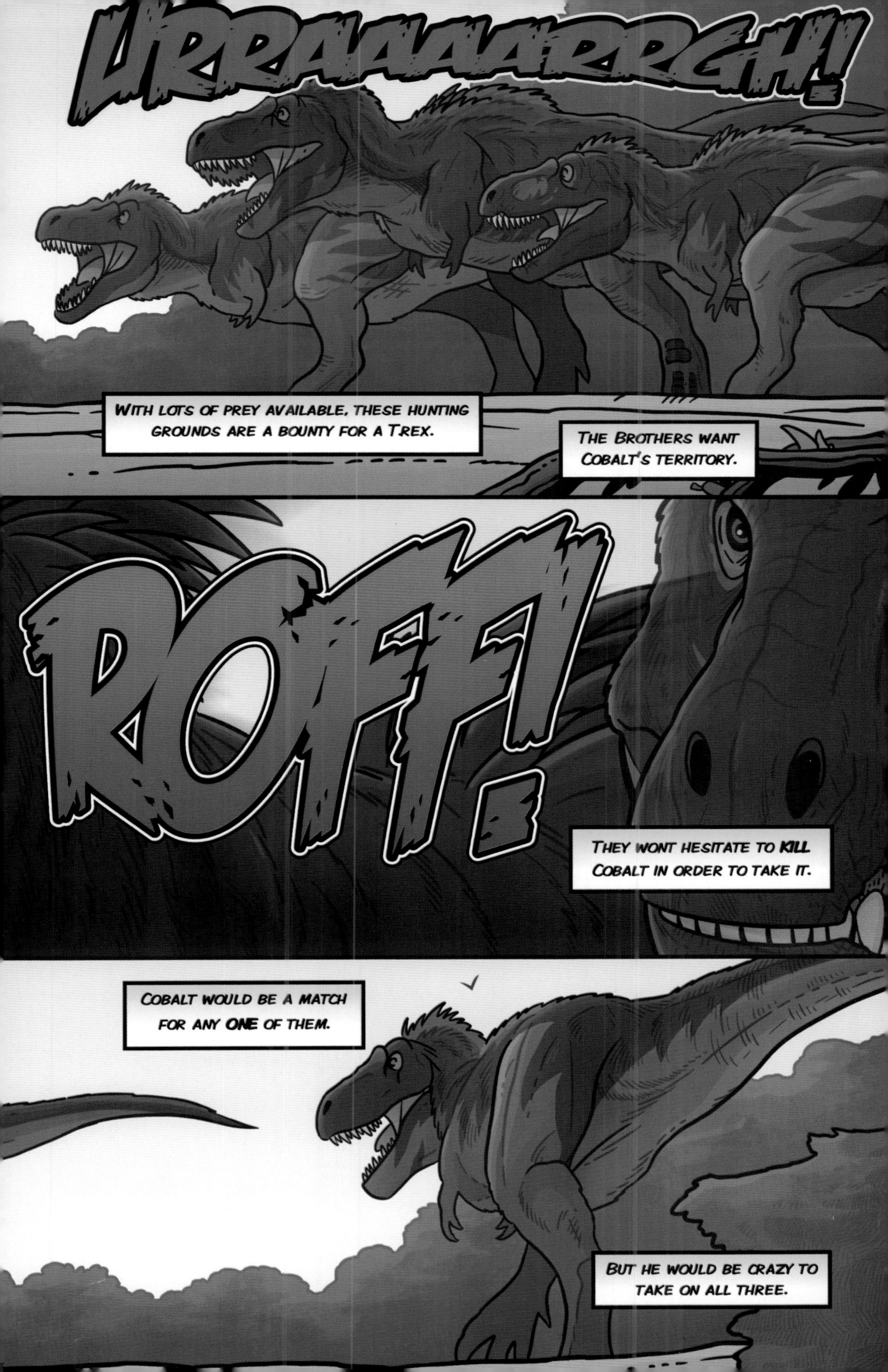
URRAAAAARRGH!
WITH LOTS OF PREY AVAILABLE, THESE HUNTING GROUNDS ARE A BOUNTY FOR A T.REX.
THE BROTHERS WANT COBALT'S TERRITORY.
ROFF!
THEY WONT HESITATE TO KILL COBALT IN ORDER TO TAKE IT.
COBALT WOULD BE A MATCH FOR ANY ONE OF THEM.
BUT HE WOULD BE CRAZY TO TAKE ON ALL THREE.

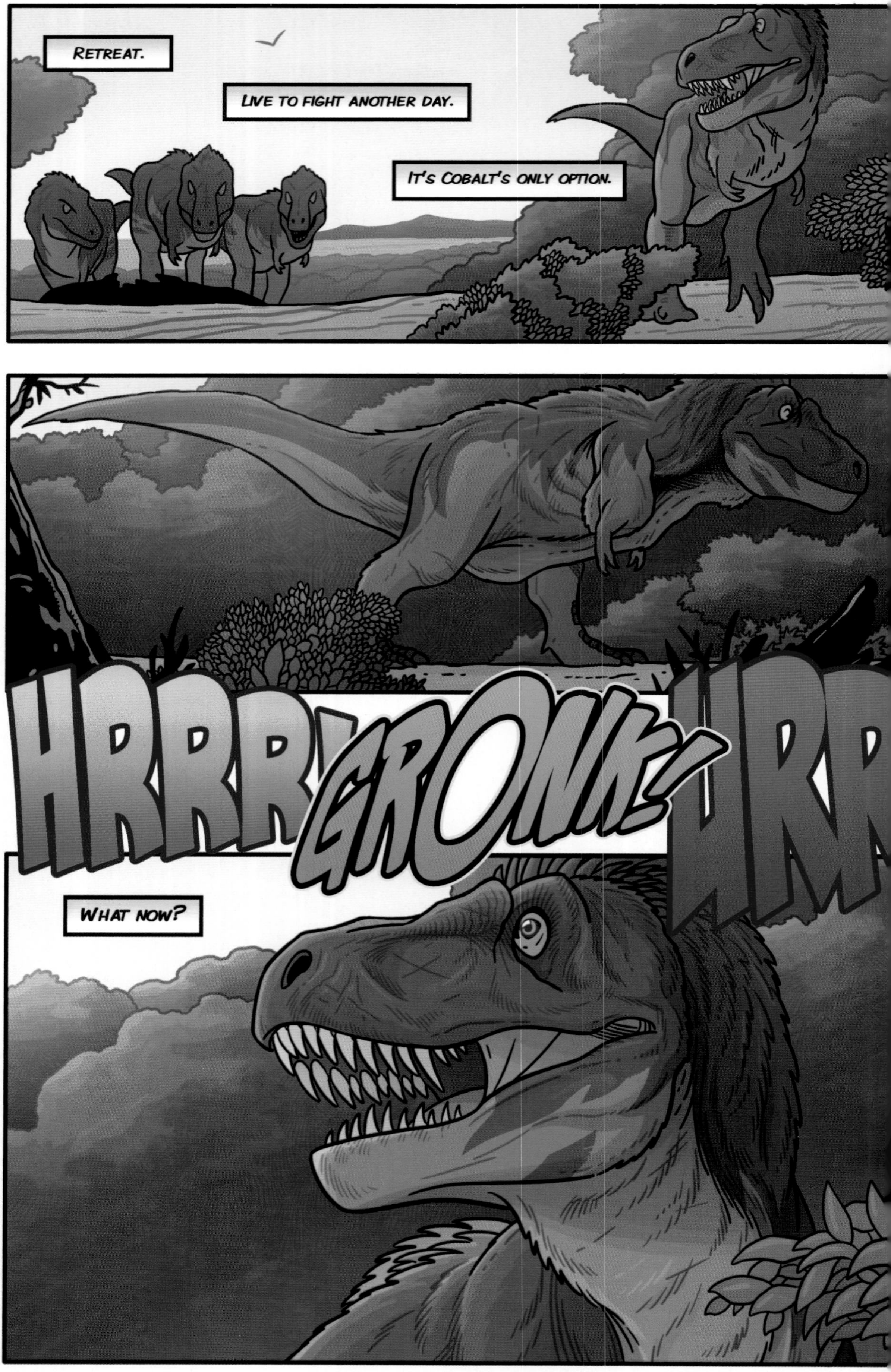
RETREAT.
LIVE TO FIGHT ANOTHER DAY.
IT'S COBALT'S ONLY OPTION.
HRRR
GRONK!
HRR
WHAT NOW?

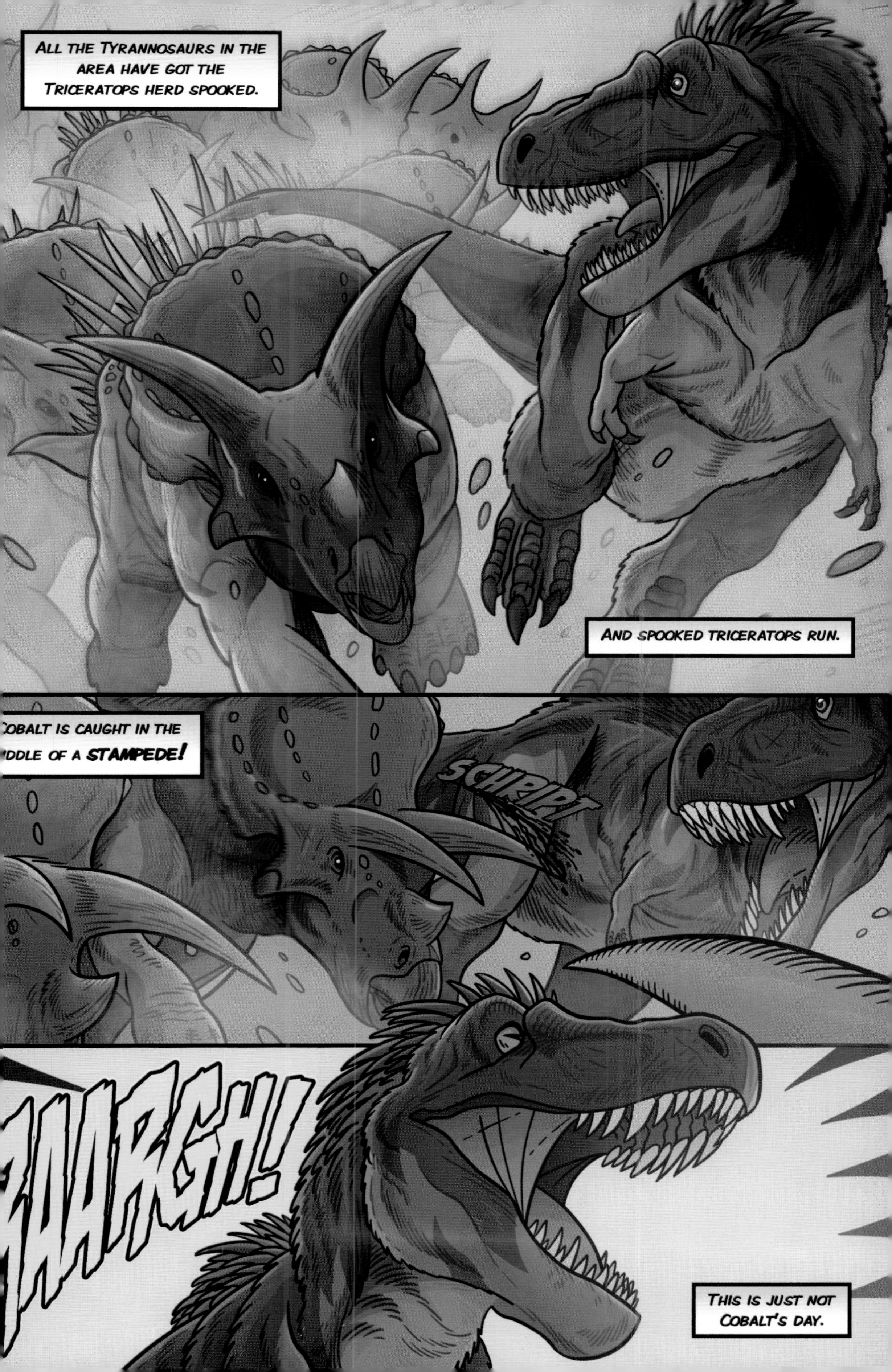
ALL THE TYRANNOSAURS IN THE AREA HAVE GOT THE TRICERATOPS HERD SPOOKED.
AND SPOOKED TRICERATOPS RUN.
COBALT IS CAUGHT IN THE
IDDLE OF A STAMPEDE!
SCHRIP!
AARGH!
THIS IS JUST NOT COBALT'S DAY.

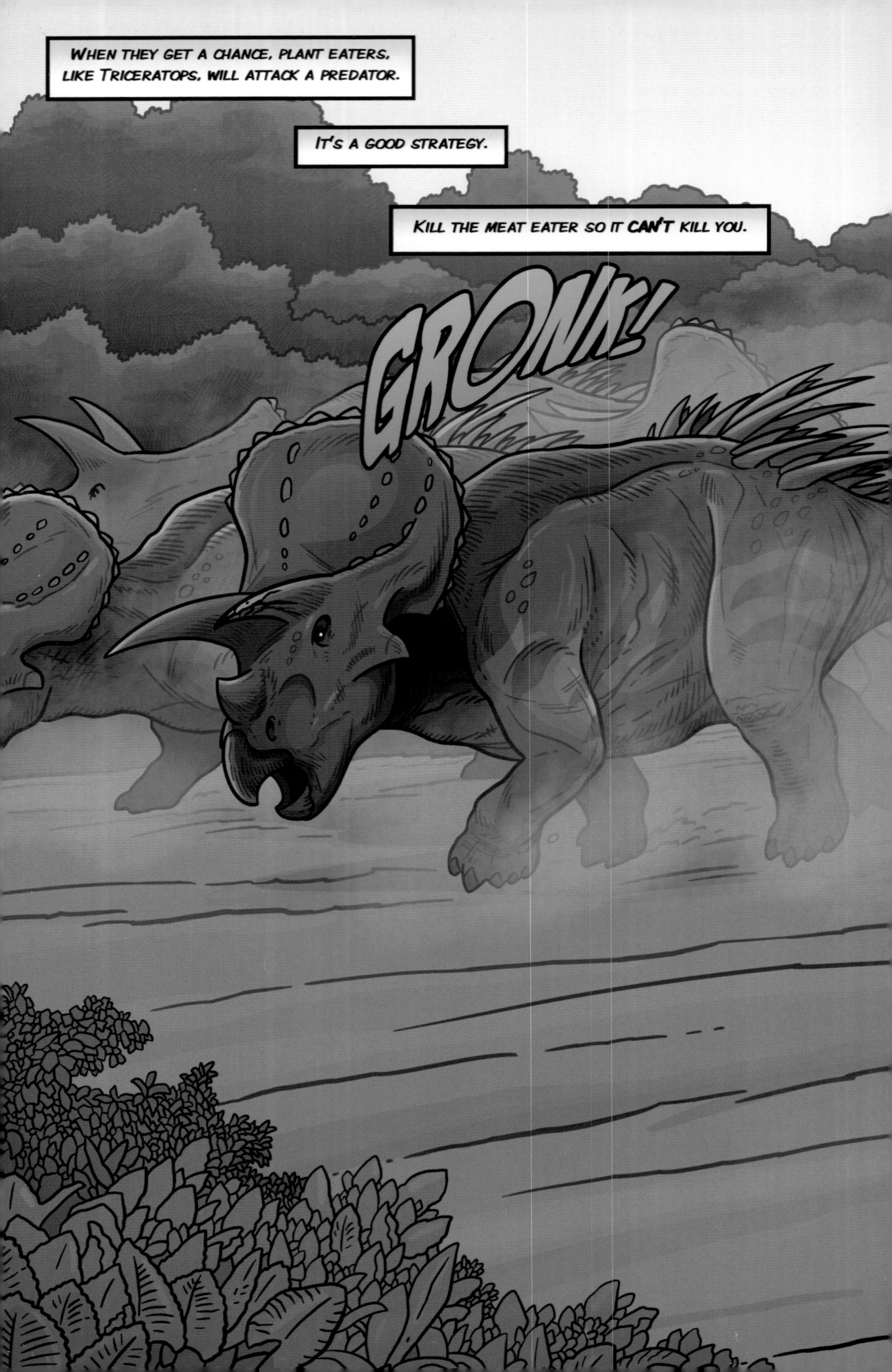
WHEN THEY GET A CHANCE, PLANT EATERS, LIKE TRICERATOPS, WILL ATTACK A PREDATOR.
IT'S A GOOD STRATEGY.
KILL THE MEAT EATER SO IT CAN'T KILL YOU.
GRONK!

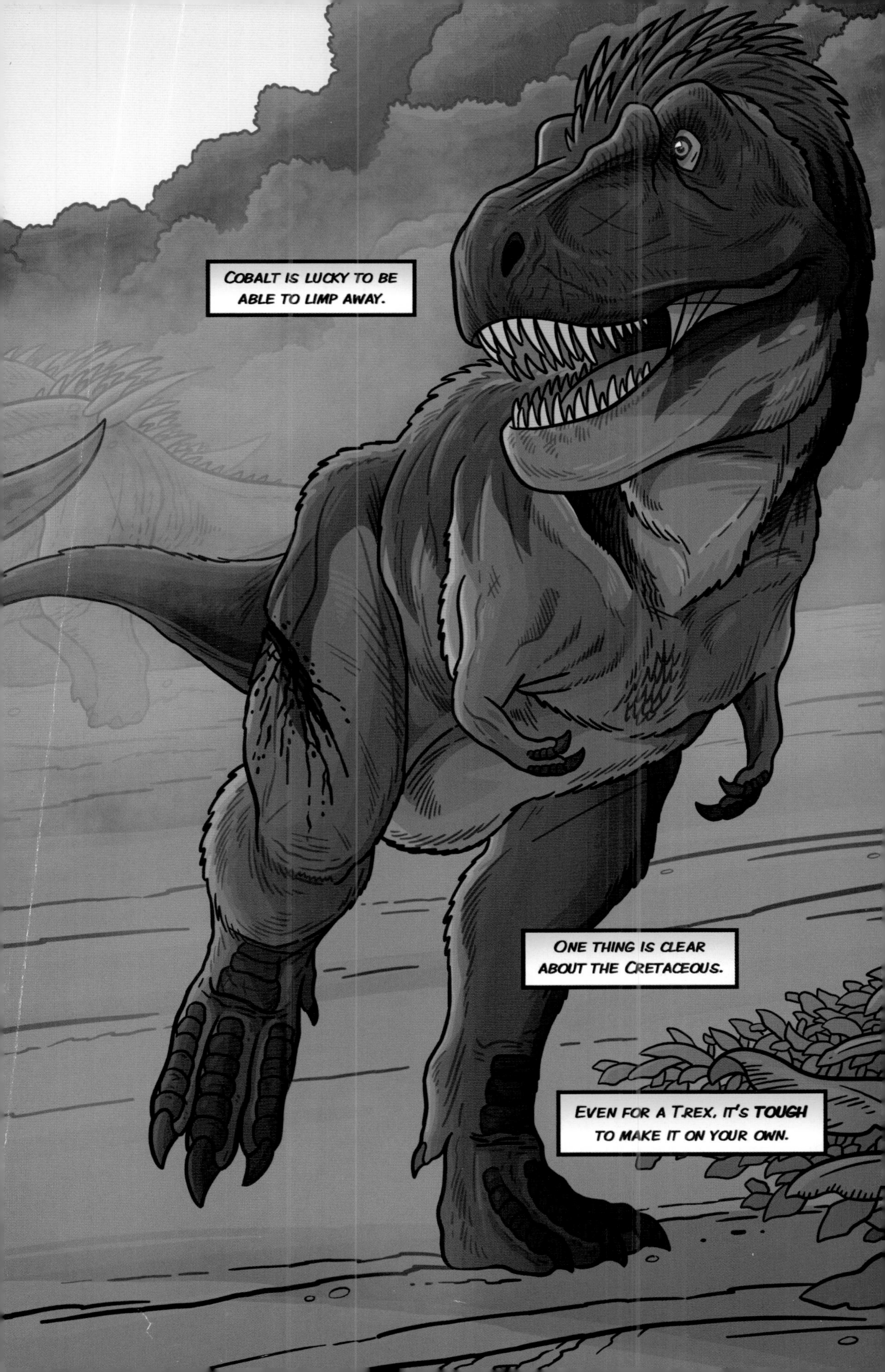
COBALT IS LUCKY TO BE ABLE TO LIMP AWAY.
ONE THING IS CLEAR ABOUT THE CRETACEOUS.
EVEN FOR A T.REX, IT'S TOUGH TO MAKE IT ON YOUR OWN.

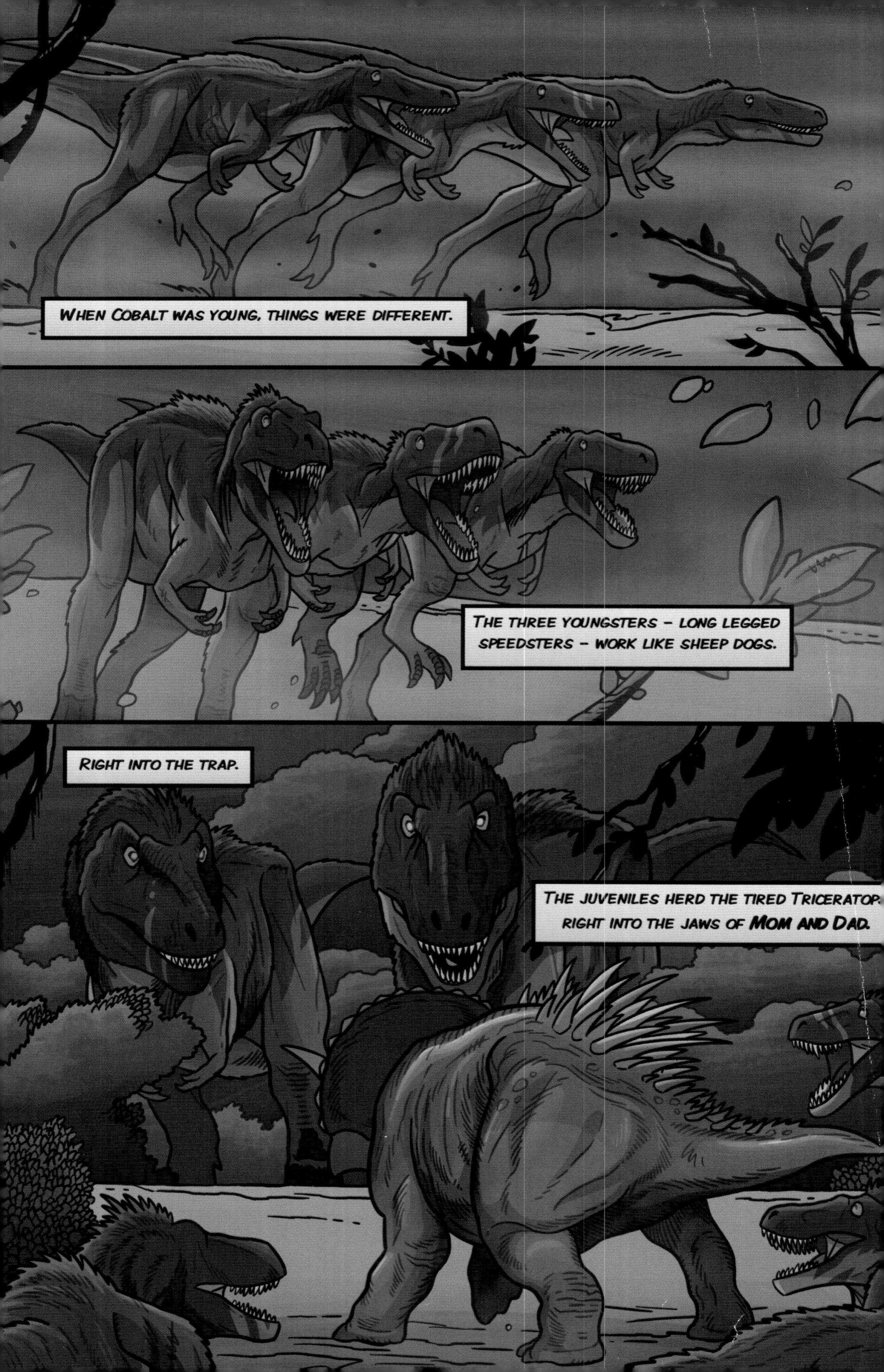
WHEN COBALT WAS YOUNG, THINGS WERE DIFFERENT.
THE THREE YOUNGSTERS - LONG LEGGED SPEEDSTERS - WORK LIKE SHEEP DOGS.
RIGHT INTO THE TRAP.
THE JUVENILES HERD THE TIRED TRICERATOPS RIGHT INTO THE JAWS OF MOM AND DAD.

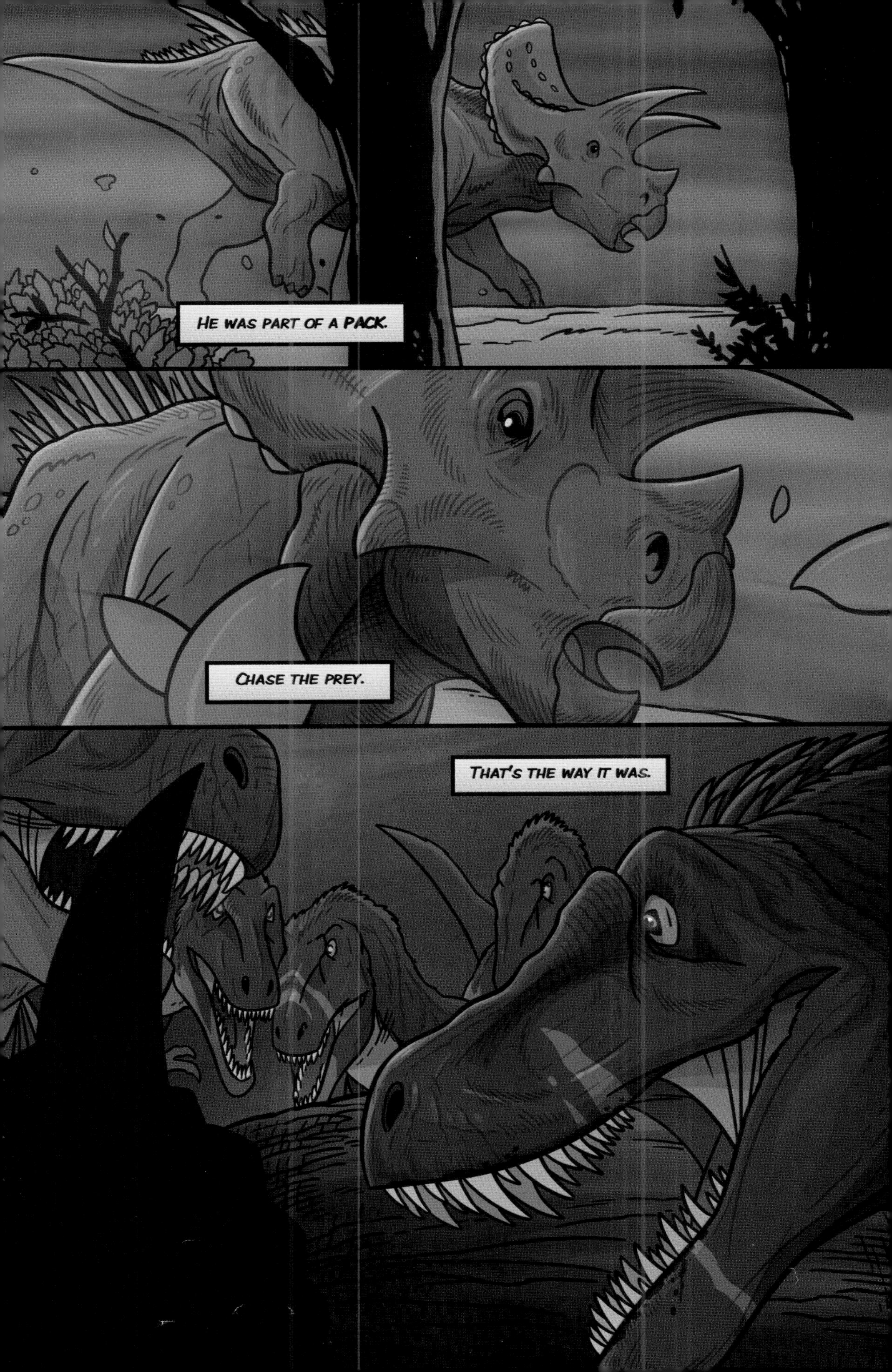

HE WAS PART OF A PACK.
CHASE THE PREY.
THAT'S THE WAY IT WAS.

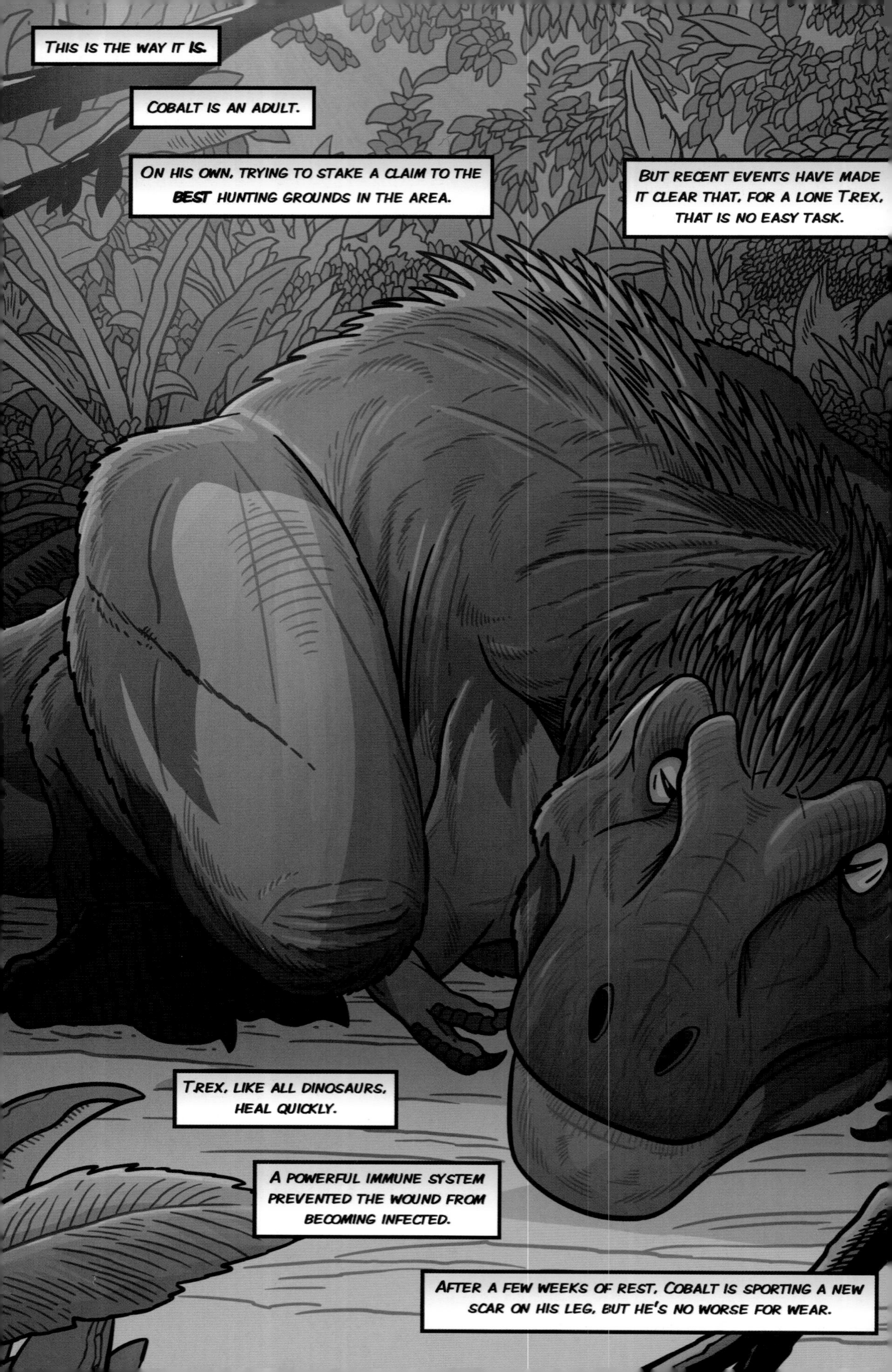
THIS IS THE WAY IT IS.
COBALT IS AN ADULT.
ON HIS OWN, TRYING TO STAKE A CLAIM TO THE BEST HUNTING GROUNDS IN THE AREA.
BUT RECENT EVENTS HAVE MADE IT CLEAR THAT, FOR A LONE T.REX, THAT IS NO EASY TASK.
T.REX, LIKE ALL DINOSAURS, HEAL QUICKLY.
A POWERFUL IMMUNE SYSTEM PREVENTED THE WOUND FROM BECOMING INFECTED.
AFTER A FEW WEEKS OF REST, COBALT IS SPORTING A NEW SCAR ON HIS LEG, BUT HE'S NO WORSE FOR WEAR.

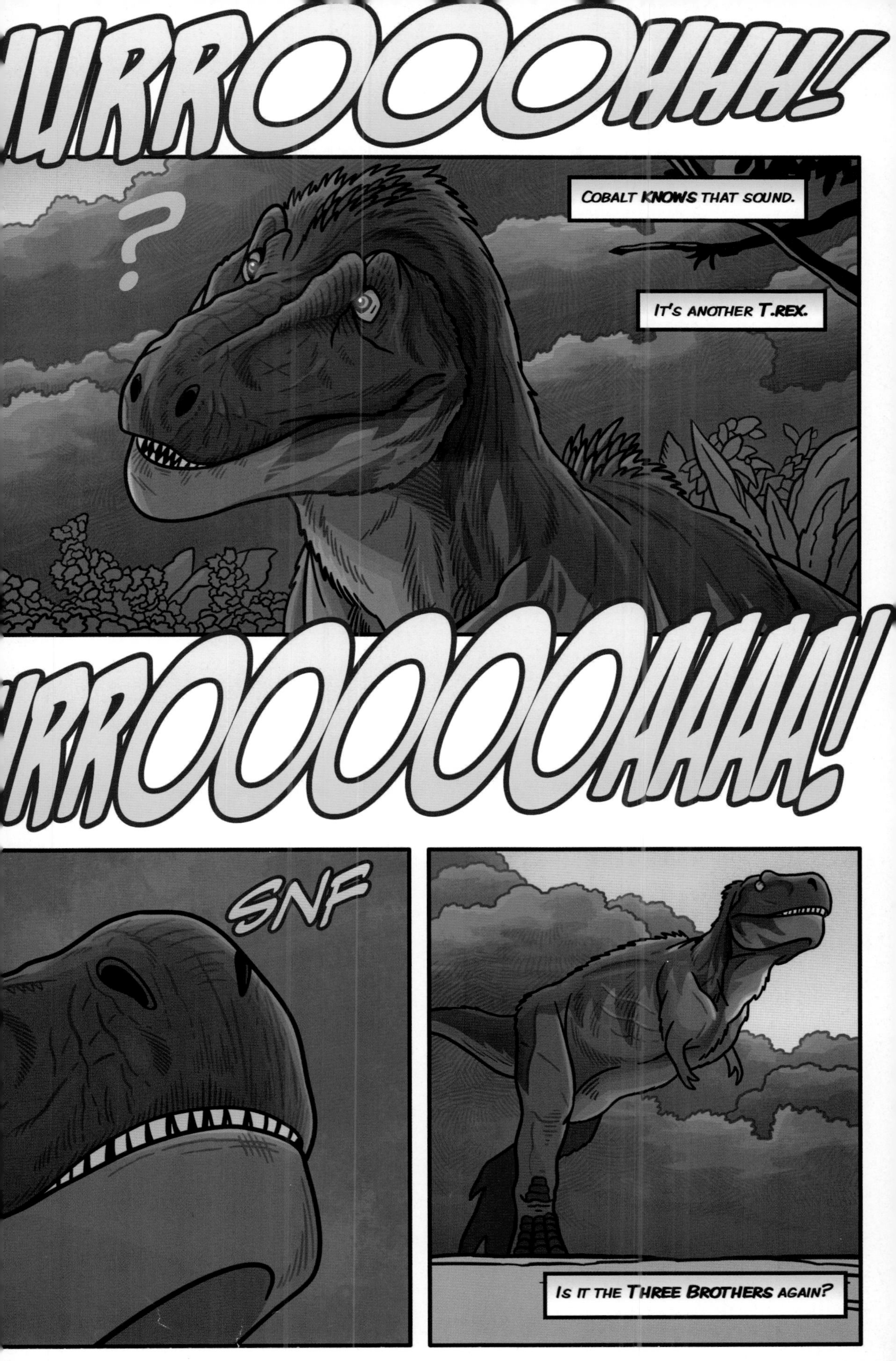
URROOOOHHH!
COBALT KNOWS THAT SOUND.
?
IT'S ANOTHER T.REX.
RROOOOOOAAAA!
SNF
IS IT THE THREE BROTHERS AGAIN?

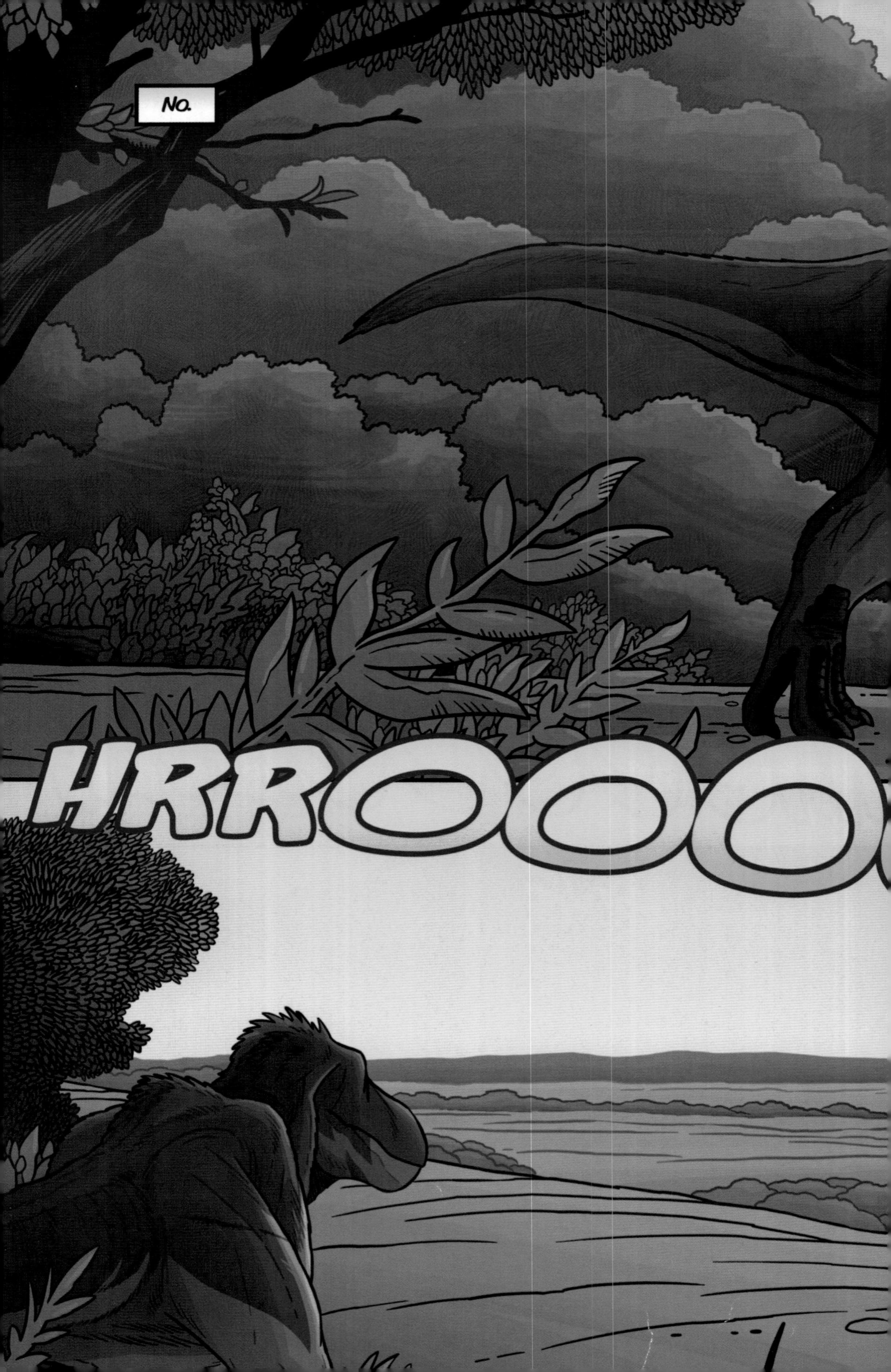
No.
HRROOO

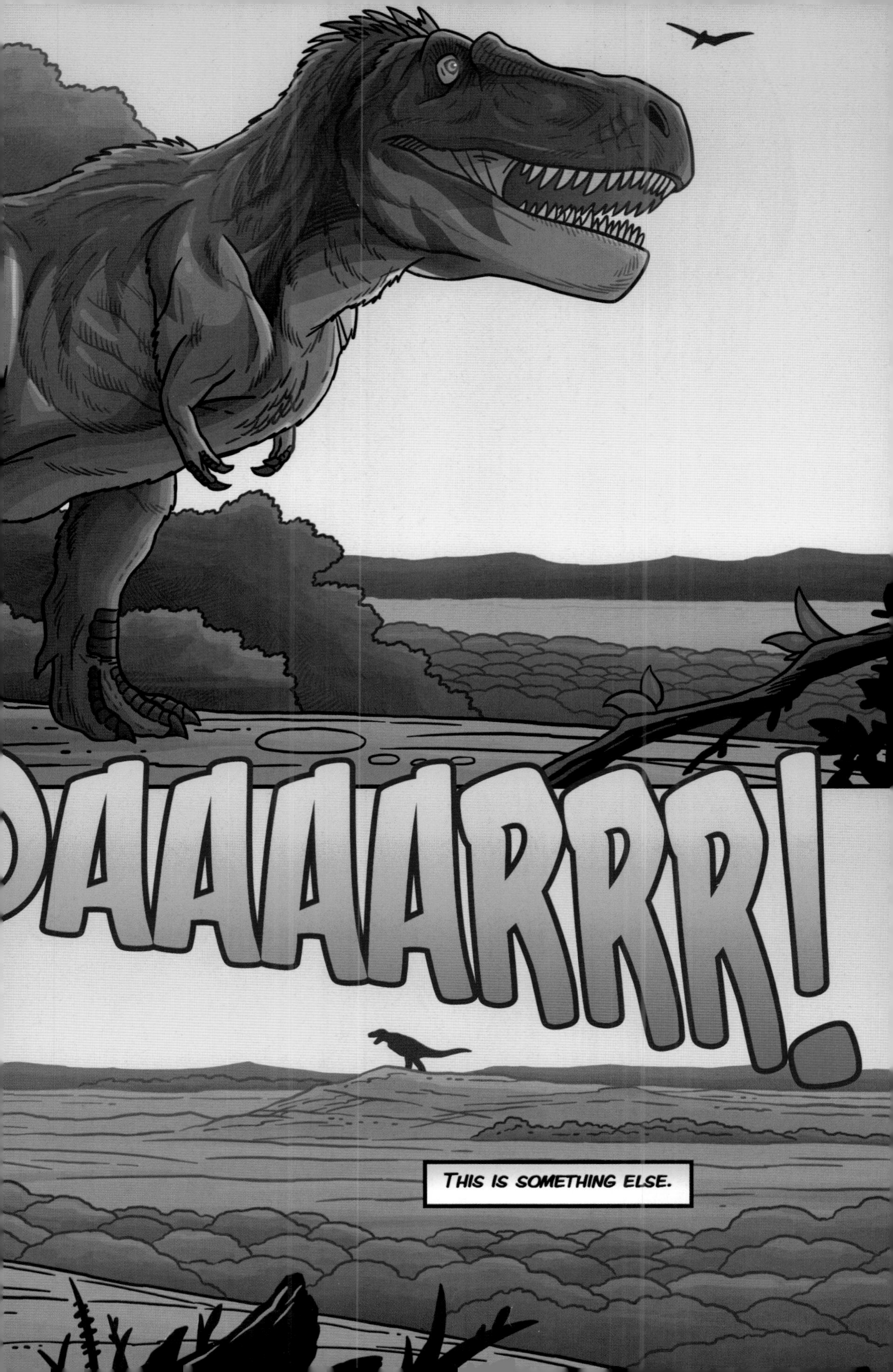
AAAARRR!
THIS IS SOMETHING ELSE.

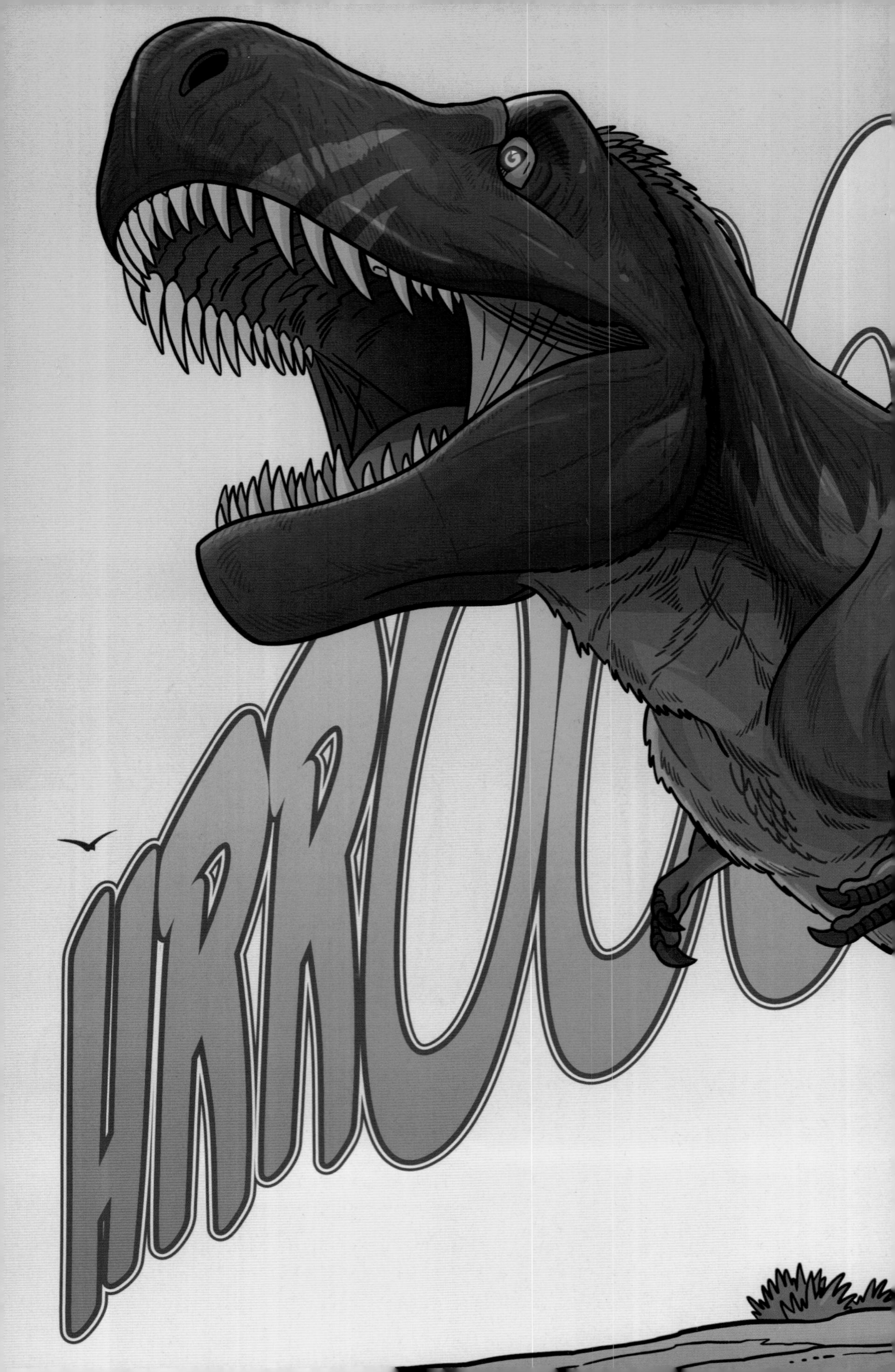

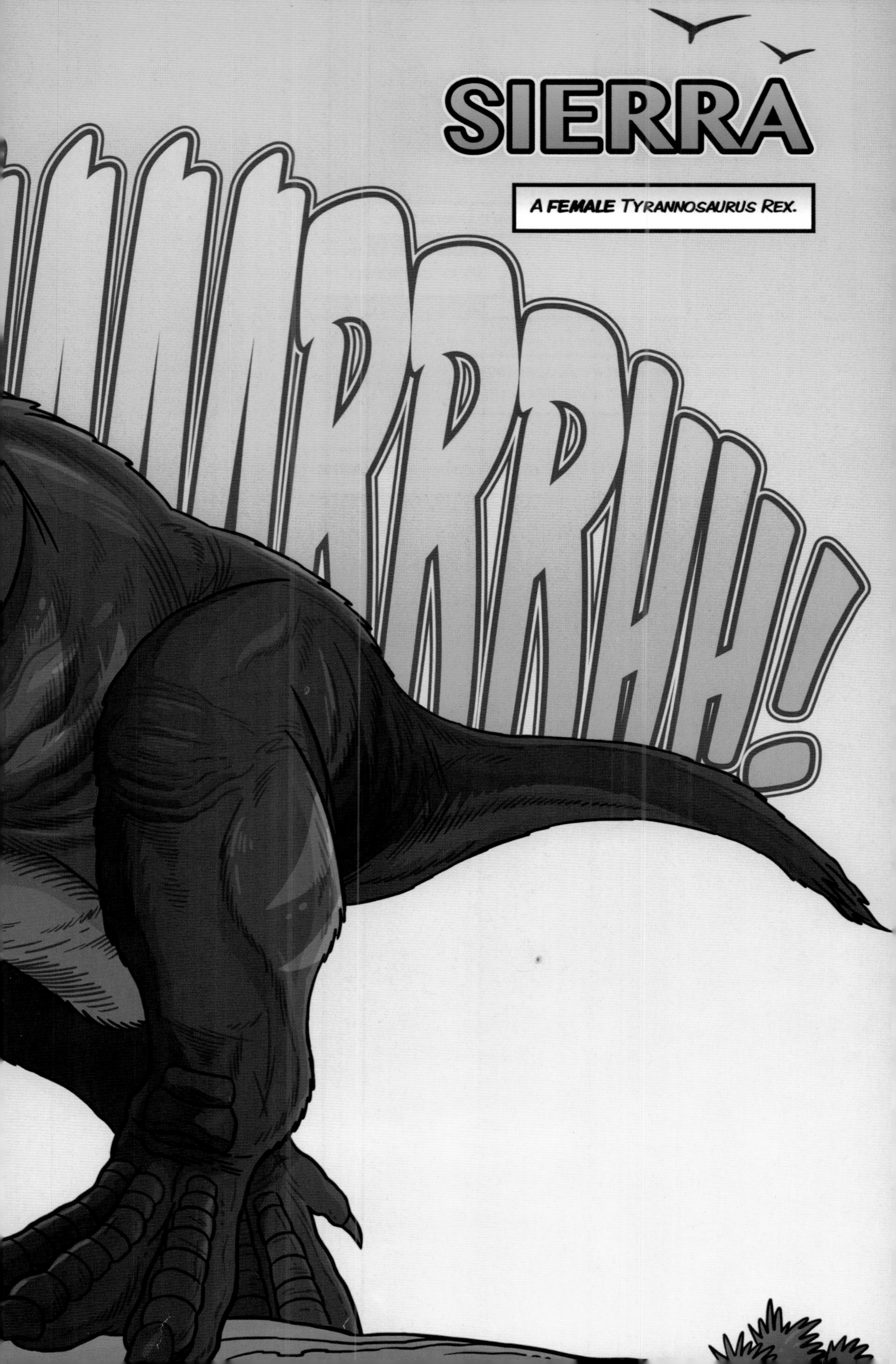
SIERRA
A FEMALE TYRANNOSAURUS REX.

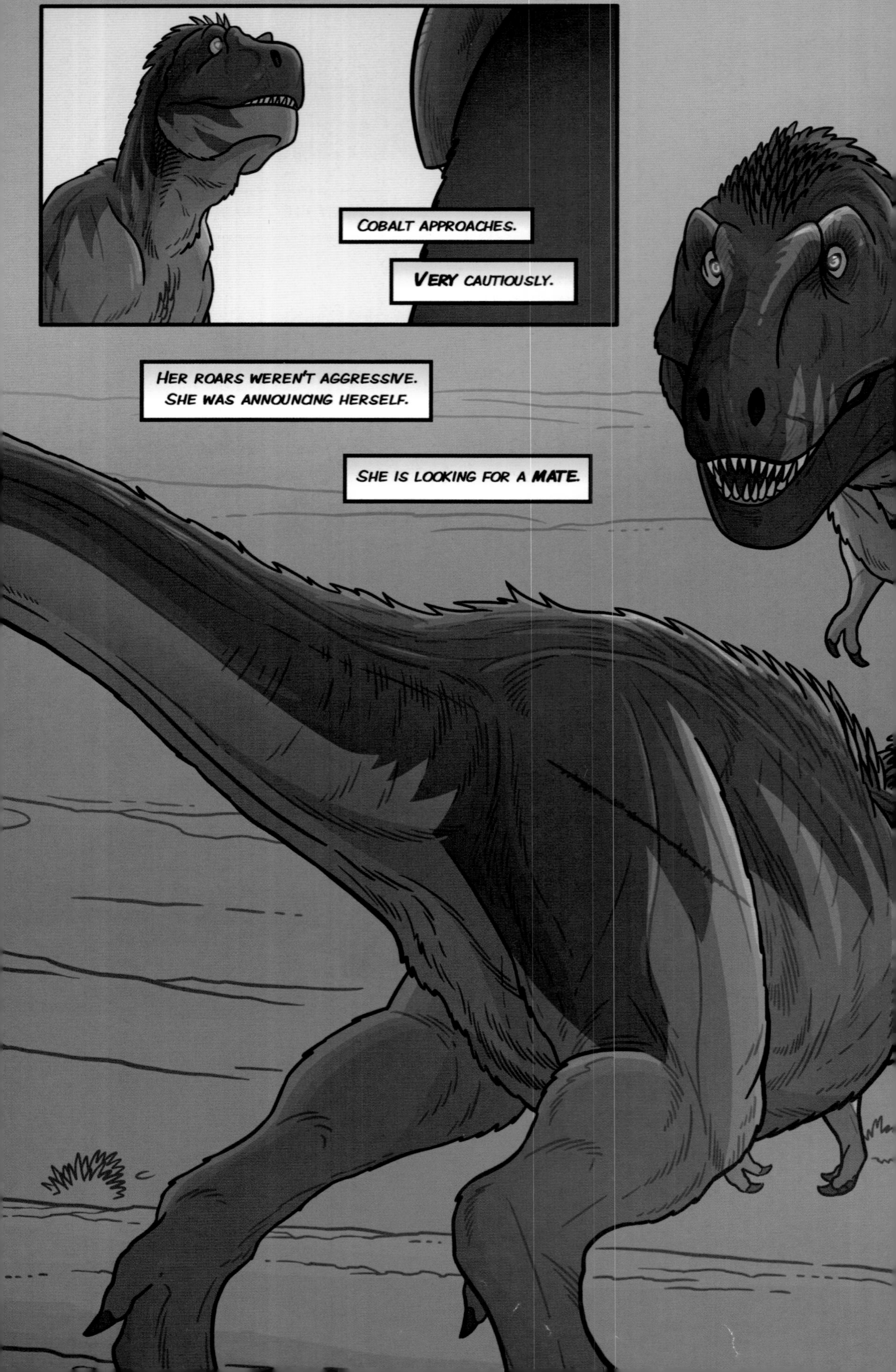

COBALT APPROACHES.
VERY CAUTIOUSLY.
HER ROARS WEREN'T AGGRESSIVE. SHE WAS ANNOUNCING HERSELF.
SHE IS LOOKING FOR A MATE.

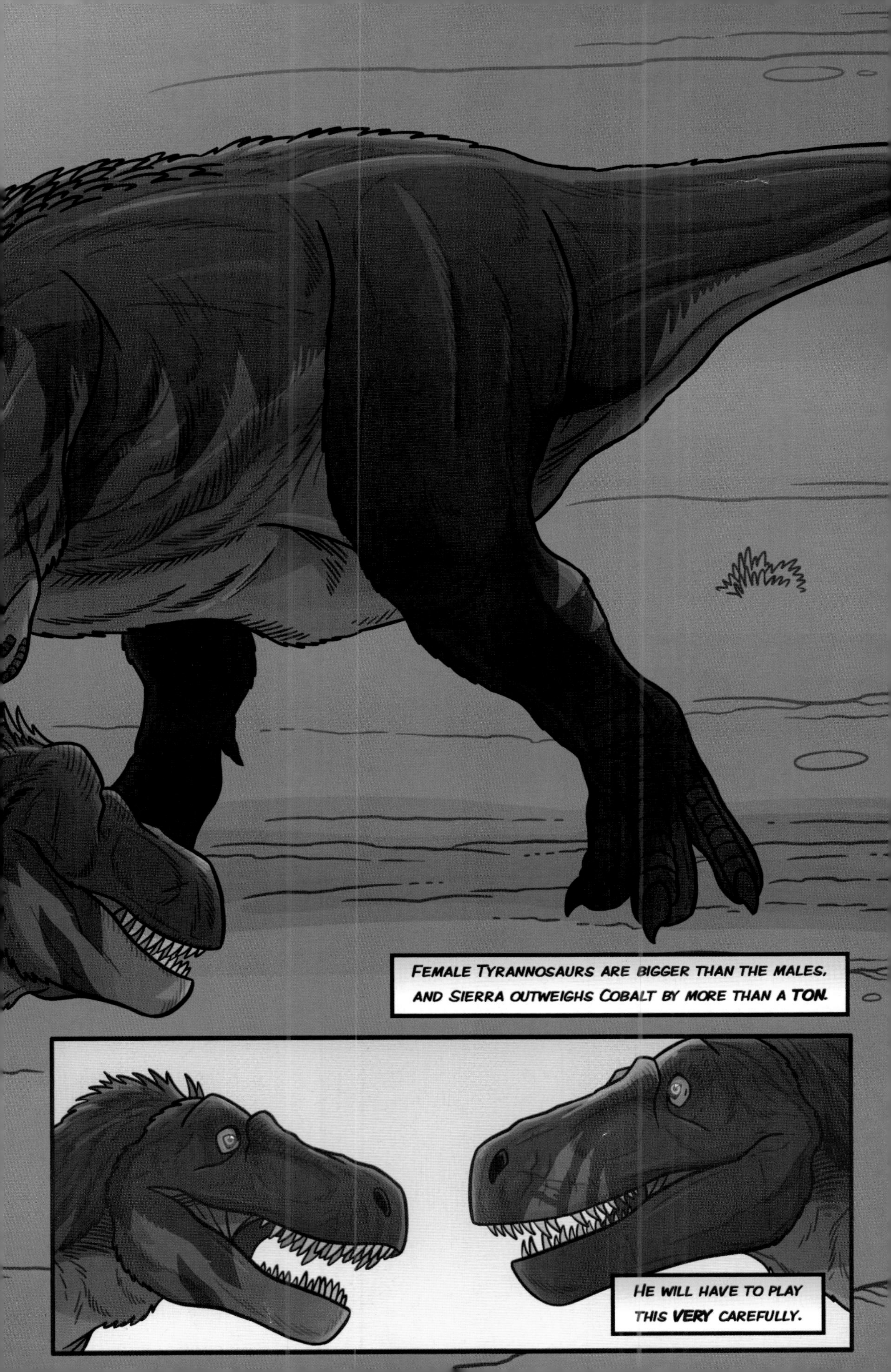
FEMALE TYRANNOSAURS ARE BIGGER THAN THE MALES, AND SIERRA OUTWEIGHS COBALT BY MORE THAN A TON.
HE WILL HAVE TO PLAY THIS VERY CAREFULLY.

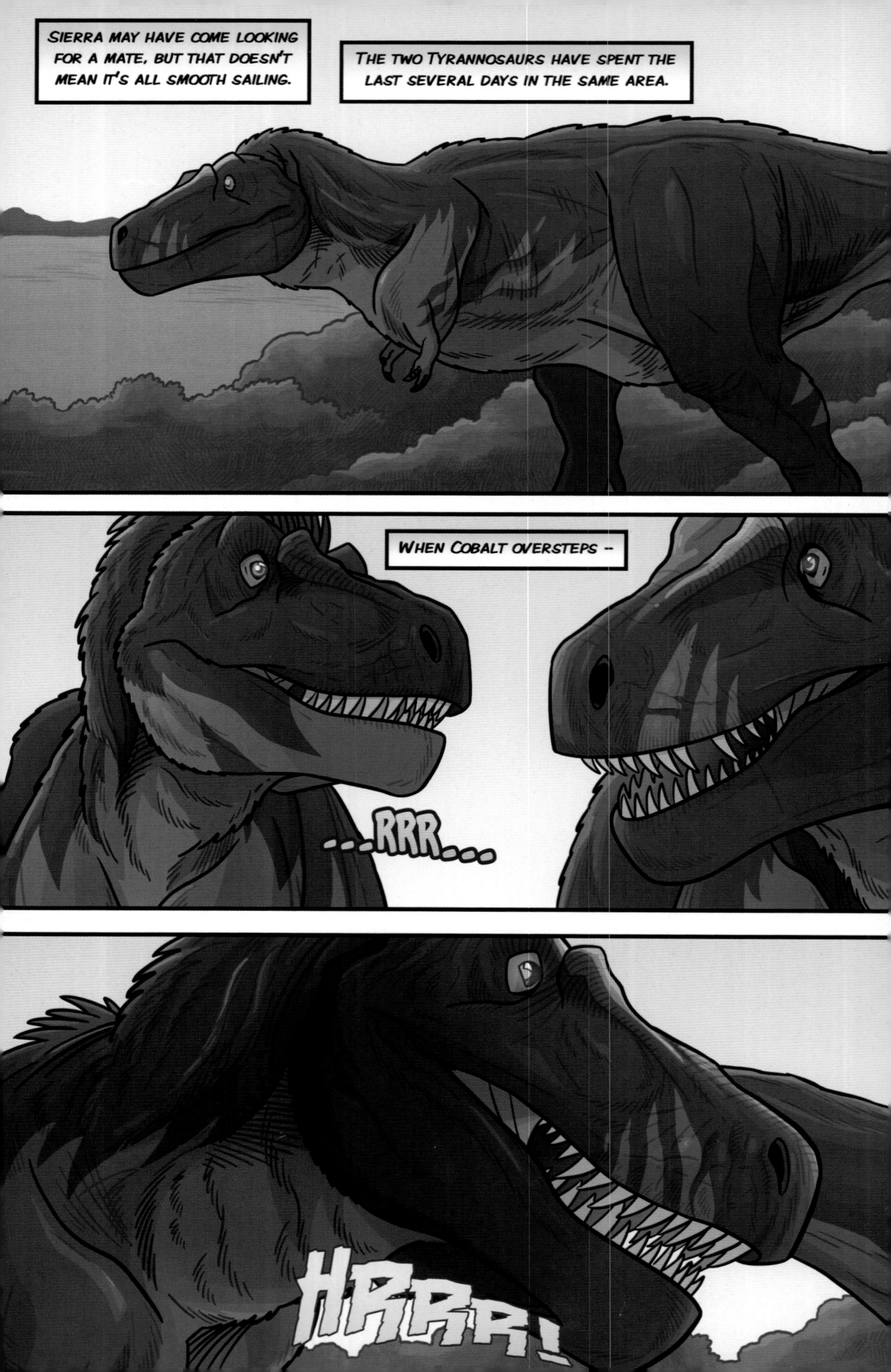
SIERRA MAY HAVE COME LOOKING FOR A MATE, BUT THAT DOESN'T MEAN IT'S ALL SMOOTH SAILING.
THE TWO TYRANNOSAURS HAVE SPENT THE LAST SEVERAL DAYS IN THE SAME AREA.
WHEN COBALT OVERSTEPS --
...RRR...
HRRR!

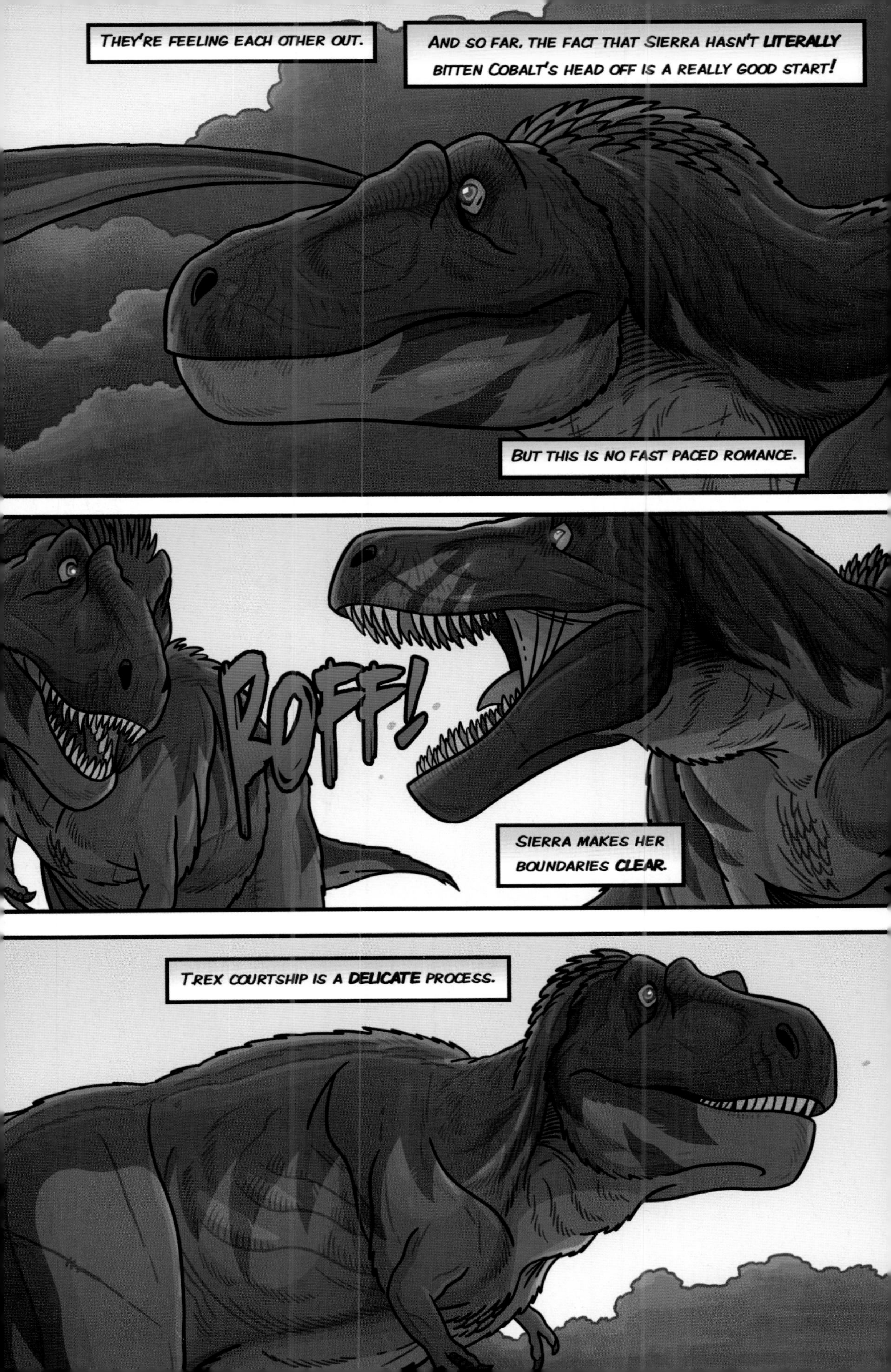
THEY'RE FEELING EACH OTHER OUT.
AND SO FAR, THE FACT THAT SIERRA HASN'T **LITERALLY** BITTEN COBALT'S HEAD OFF IS A REALLY GOOD START!
BUT THIS IS NO FAST PACED ROMANCE.
ROFF!
SIERRA MAKES HER BOUNDARIES **CLEAR**.
TREX COURTSHIP IS A **DELICATE** PROCESS.

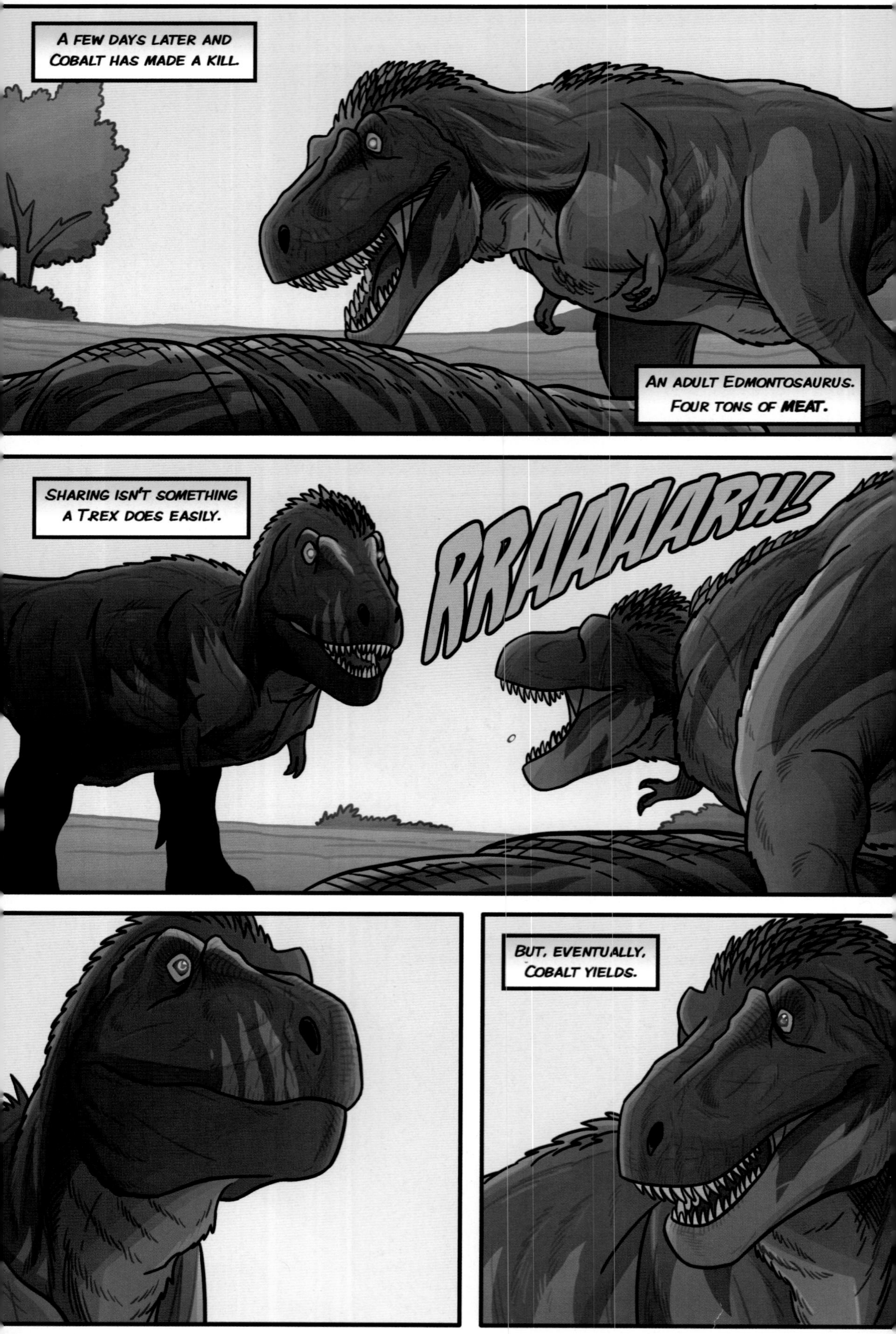
A few days later and Cobalt has made a kill.
An adult Edmontosaurus. Four tons of MEAT.
Sharing isn't something a T.rex does easily.
RRAAAAARH!
But, eventually, Cobalt yields.

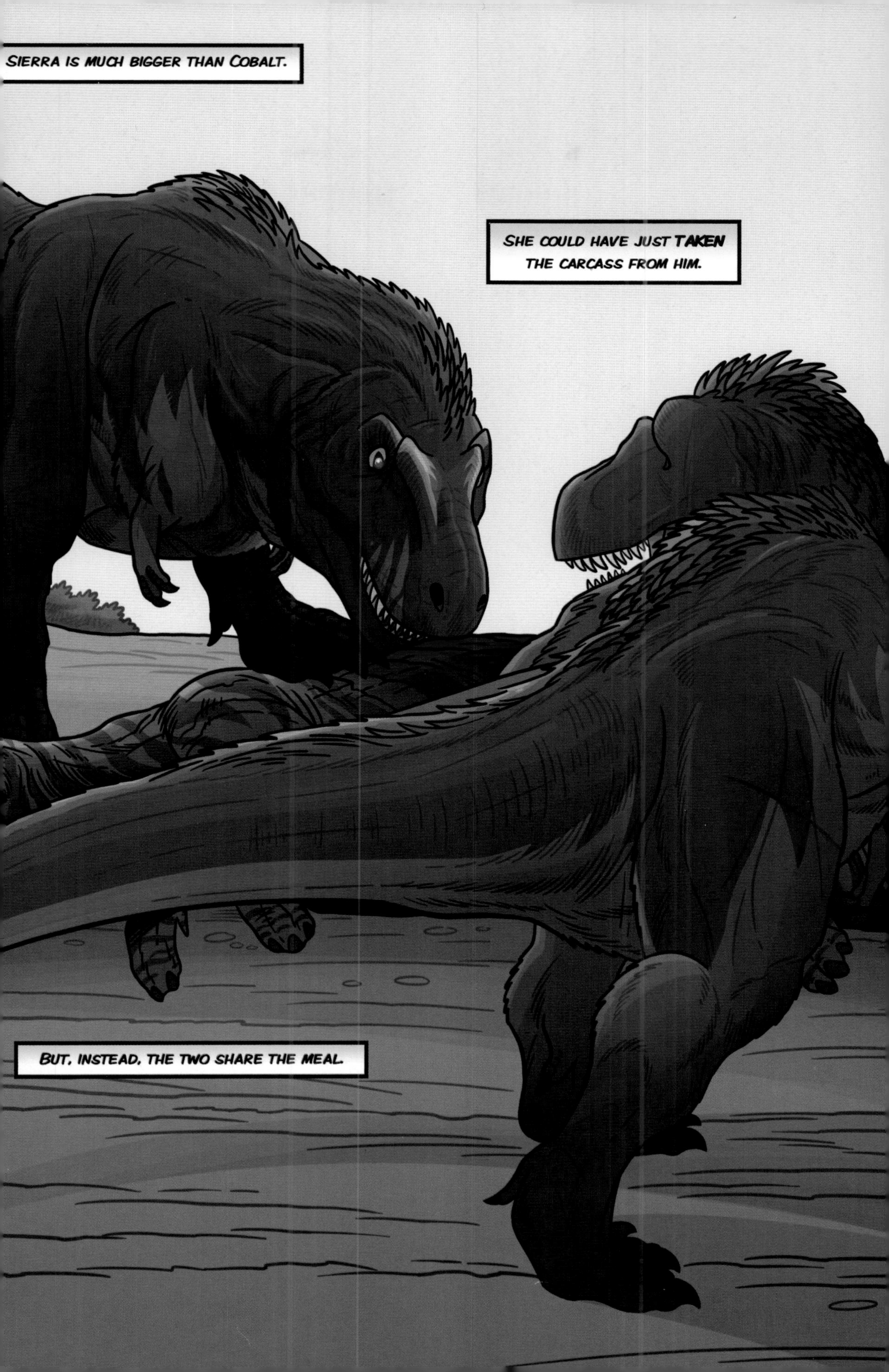
SIERRA IS MUCH BIGGER THAN COBALT.
SHE COULD HAVE JUST TAKEN THE CARCASS FROM HIM.
BUT, INSTEAD, THE TWO SHARE THE MEAL.

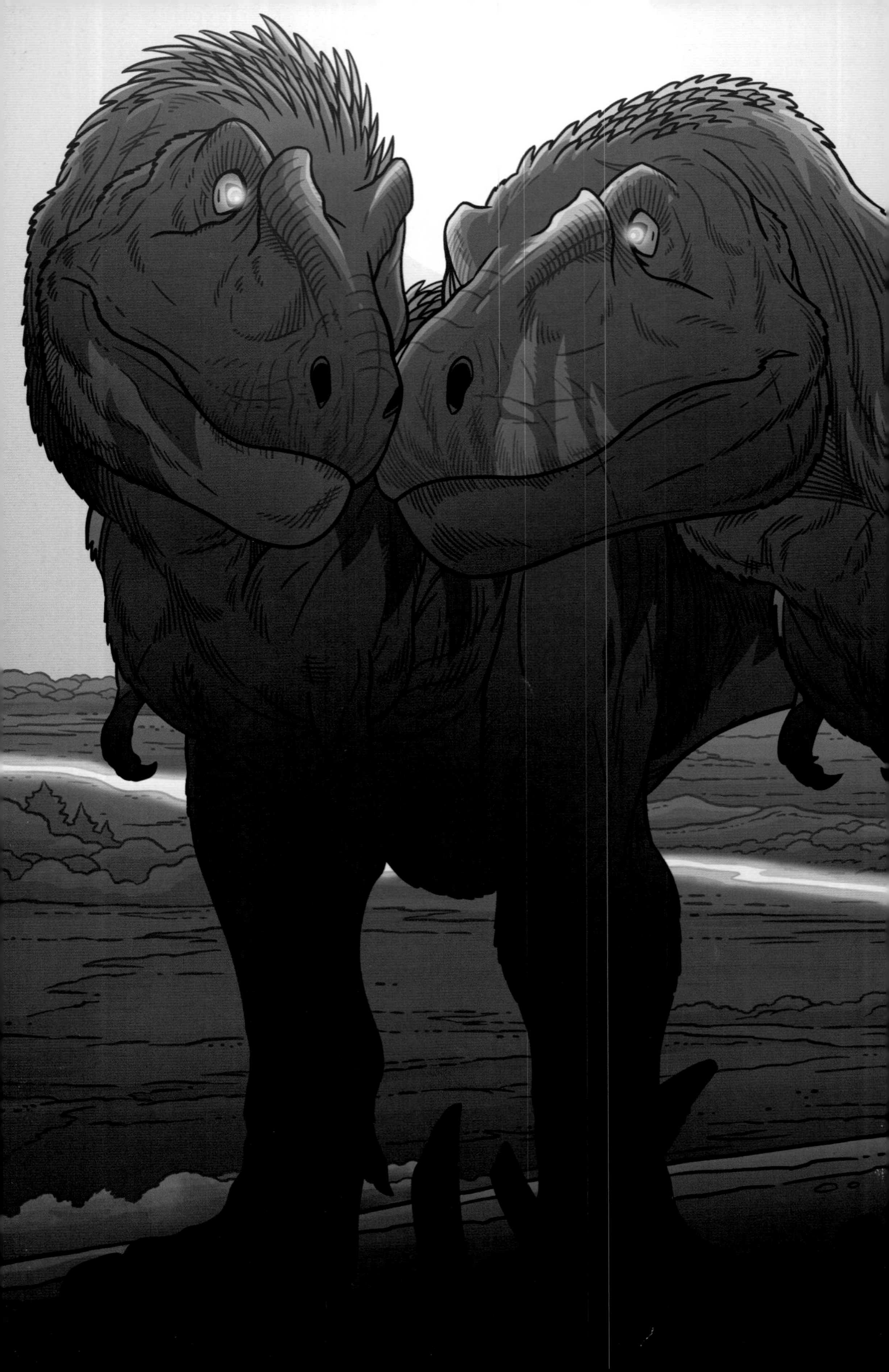

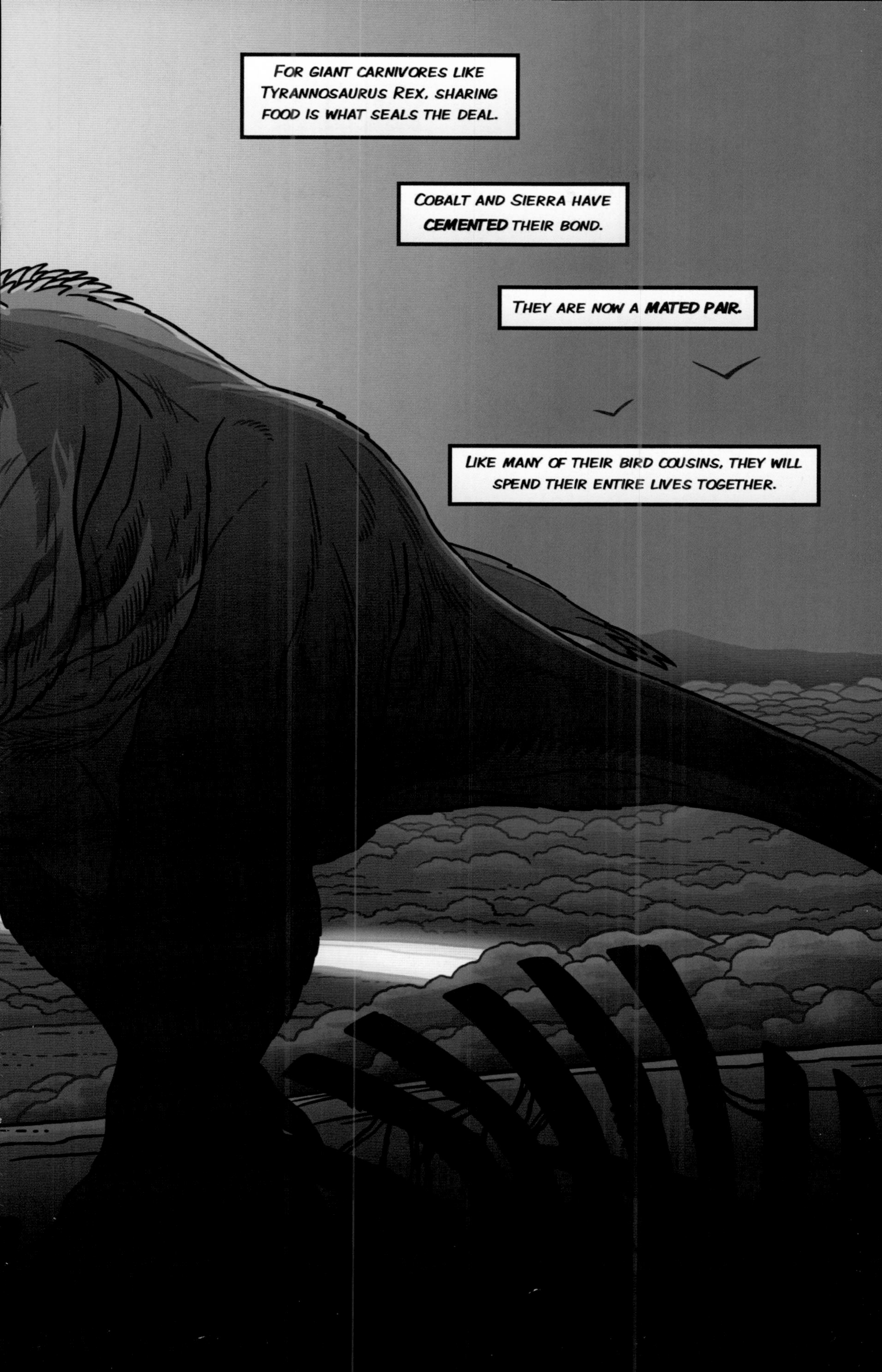
FOR GIANT CARNIVORES LIKE TYRANNOSAURUS REX, SHARING FOOD IS WHAT SEALS THE DEAL.
COBALT AND SIERRA HAVE CEMENTED THEIR BOND.
THEY ARE NOW A MATED PAIR.
LIKE MANY OF THEIR BIRD COUSINS, THEY WILL SPEND THEIR ENTIRE LIVES TOGETHER.

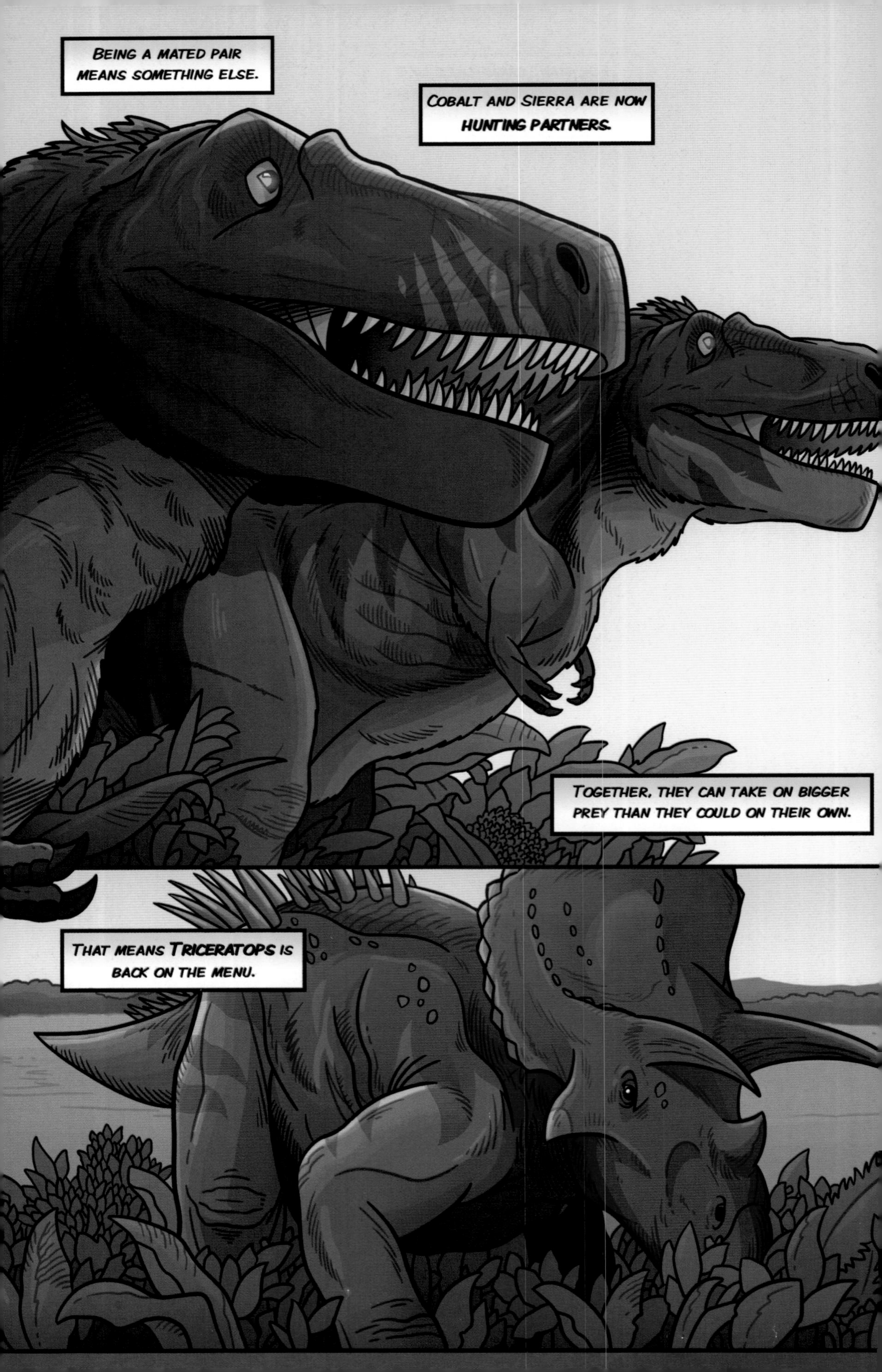
BEING A MATED PAIR MEANS SOMETHING ELSE.
COBALT AND SIERRA ARE NOW HUNTING PARTNERS.
TOGETHER, THEY CAN TAKE ON BIGGER PREY THAN THEY COULD ON THEIR OWN.
THAT MEANS TRICERATOPS IS BACK ON THE MENU.

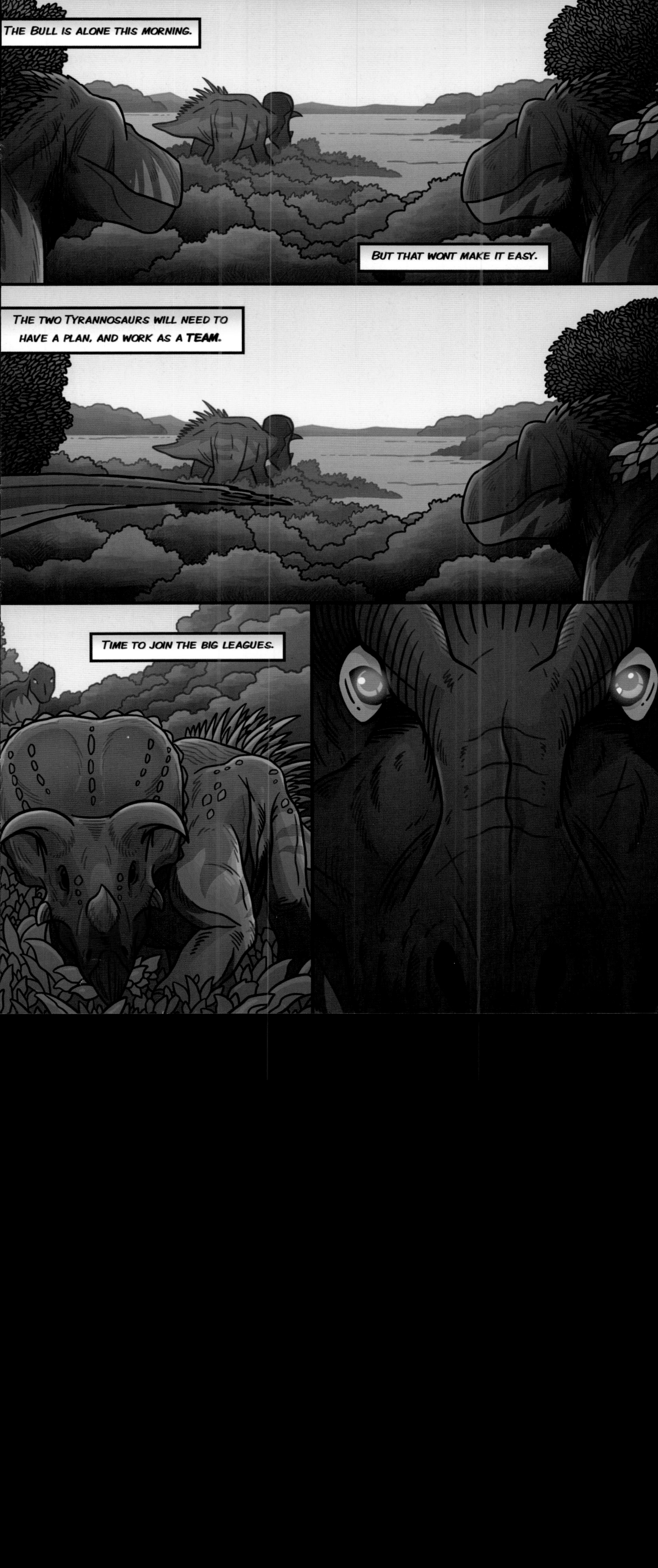
THE BULL IS ALONE THIS MORNING.
BUT THAT WONT MAKE IT EASY.
THE TWO TYRANNOSAURS WILL NEED TO HAVE A PLAN, AND WORK AS A TEAM.
TIME TO JOIN THE BIG LEAGUES.

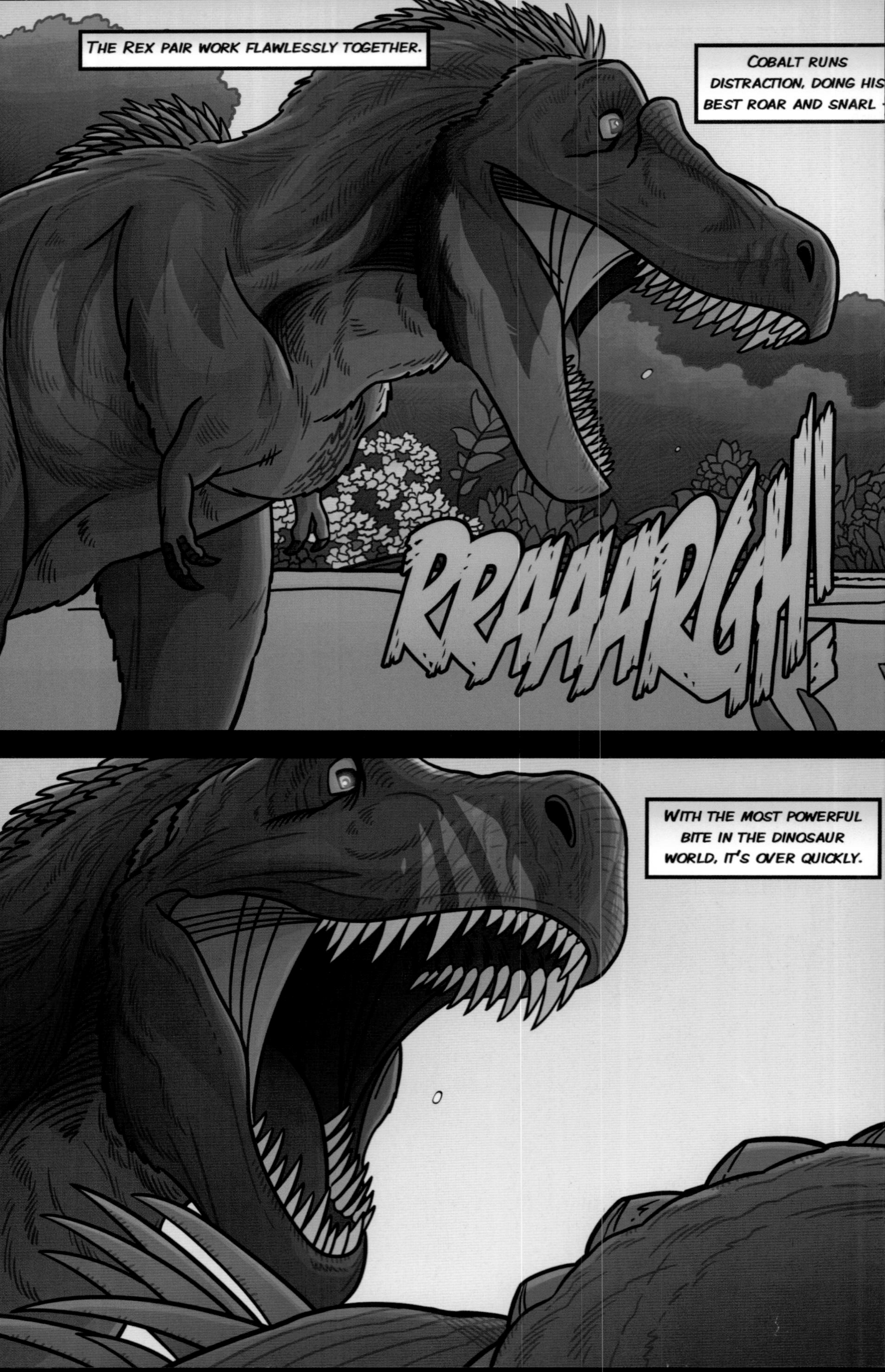
THE REX PAIR WORK FLAWLESSLY TOGETHER.
COBALT RUNS DISTRACTION, DOING HIS BEST ROAR AND SNARL
RRAAARGH!
WITH THE MOST POWERFUL BITE IN THE DINOSAUR WORLD, IT'S OVER QUICKLY.

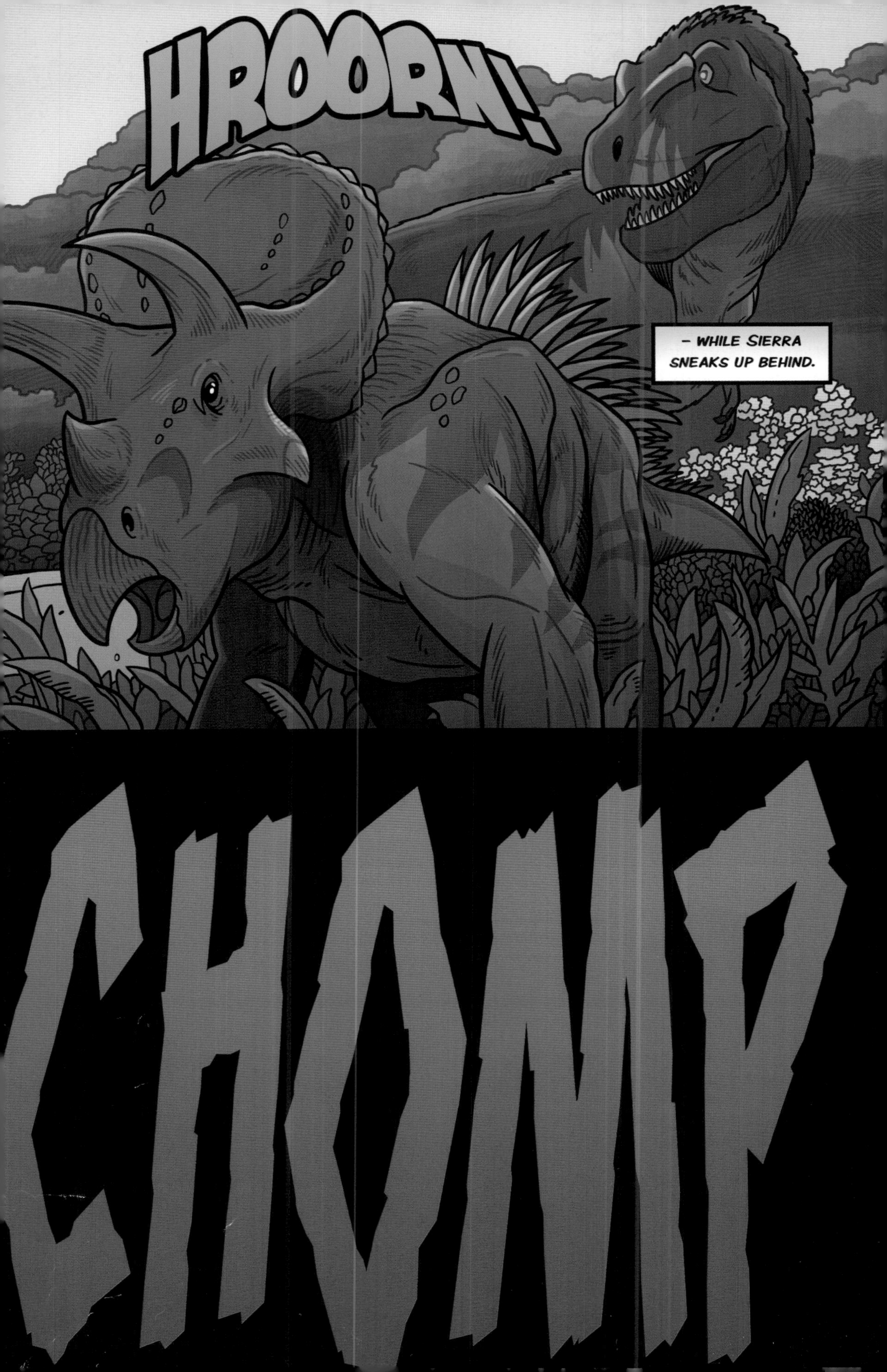
HROORN!
- WHILE SIERRA SNEAKS UP BEHIND.
CHOMP

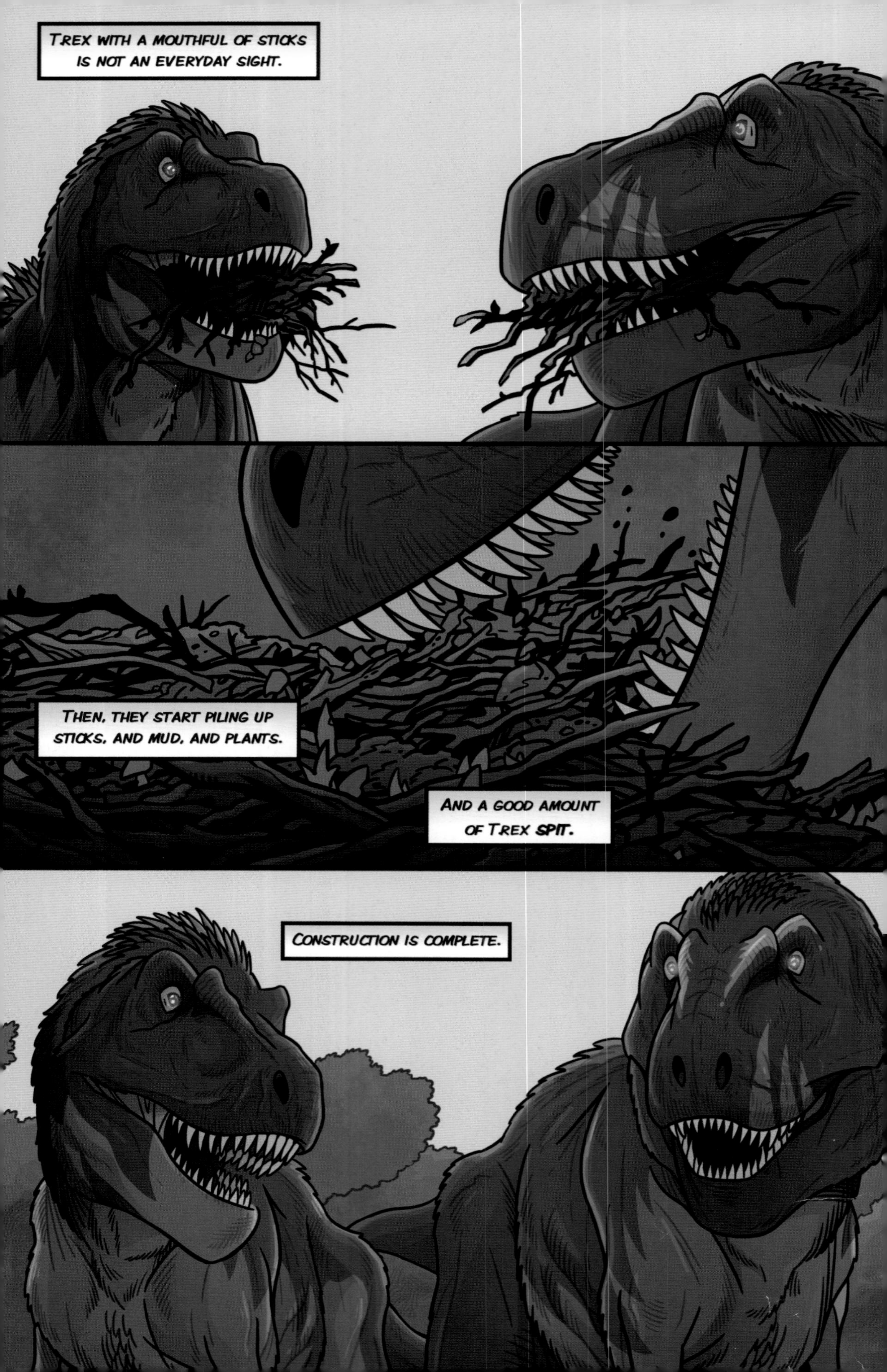
T.REX WITH A MOUTHFUL OF STICKS IS NOT AN EVERYDAY SIGHT.
THEN, THEY START PILING UP STICKS, AND MUD, AND PLANTS.
AND A GOOD AMOUNT OF T.REX SPIT.
CONSTRUCTION IS COMPLETE.

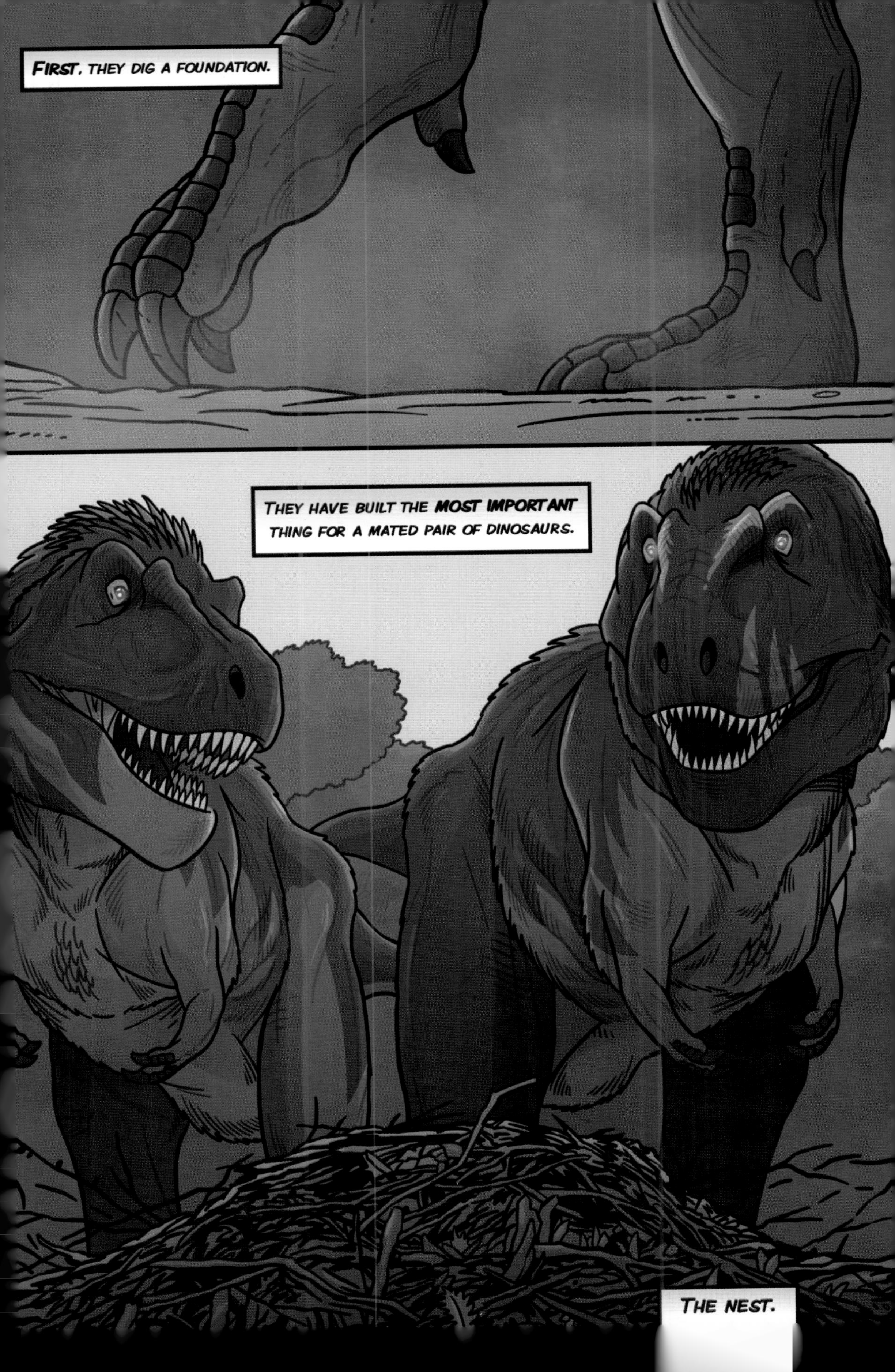
FIRST, THEY DIG A FOUNDATION.
THEY HAVE BUILT THE MOST IMPORTANT THING FOR A MATED PAIR OF DINOSAURS.
THE NEST.

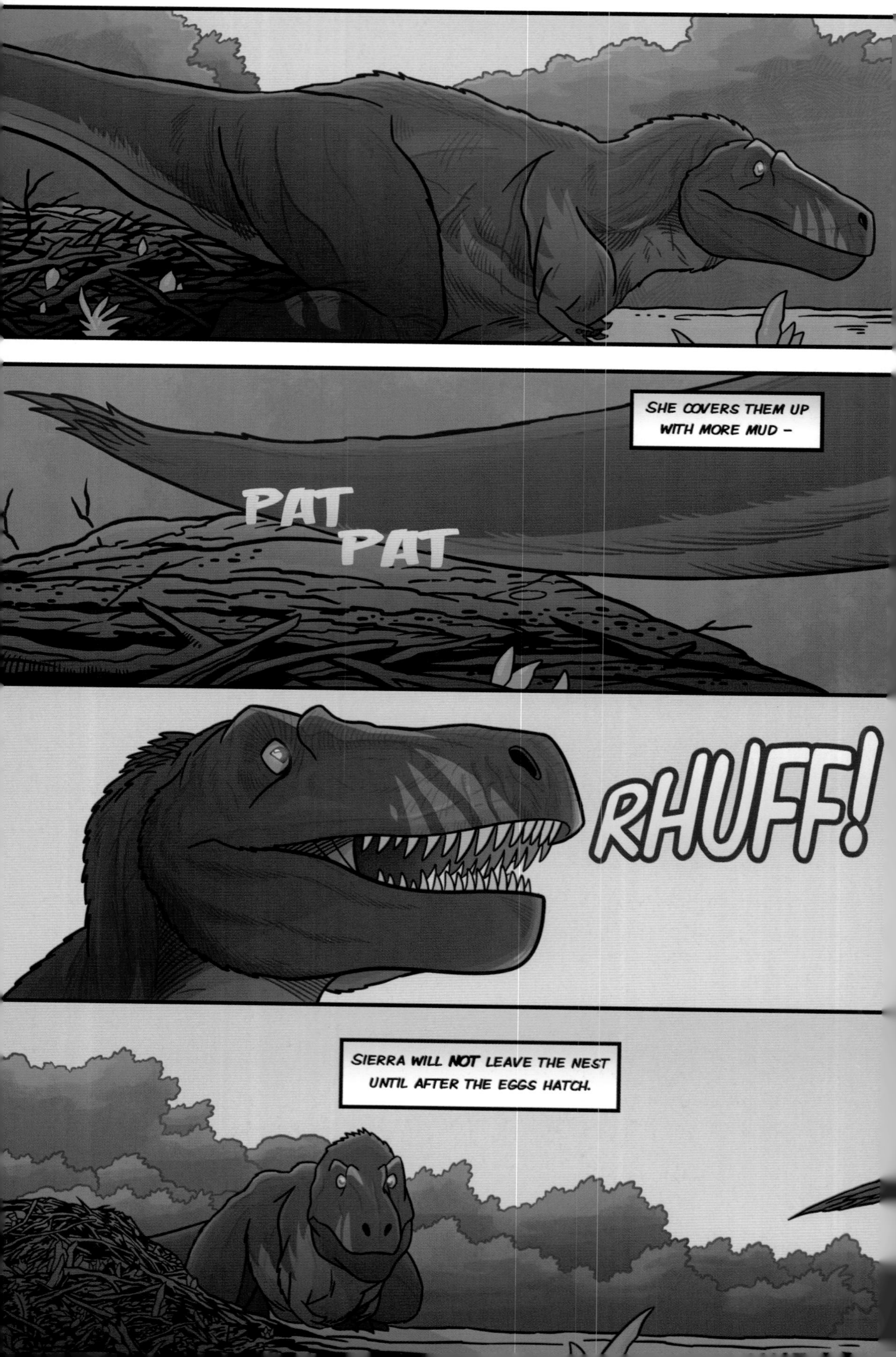
SHE COVERS THEM UP WITH MORE MUD –
PAT
PAT
RHUFF!
SIERRA WILL NOT LEAVE THE NEST UNTIL AFTER THE EGGS HATCH.

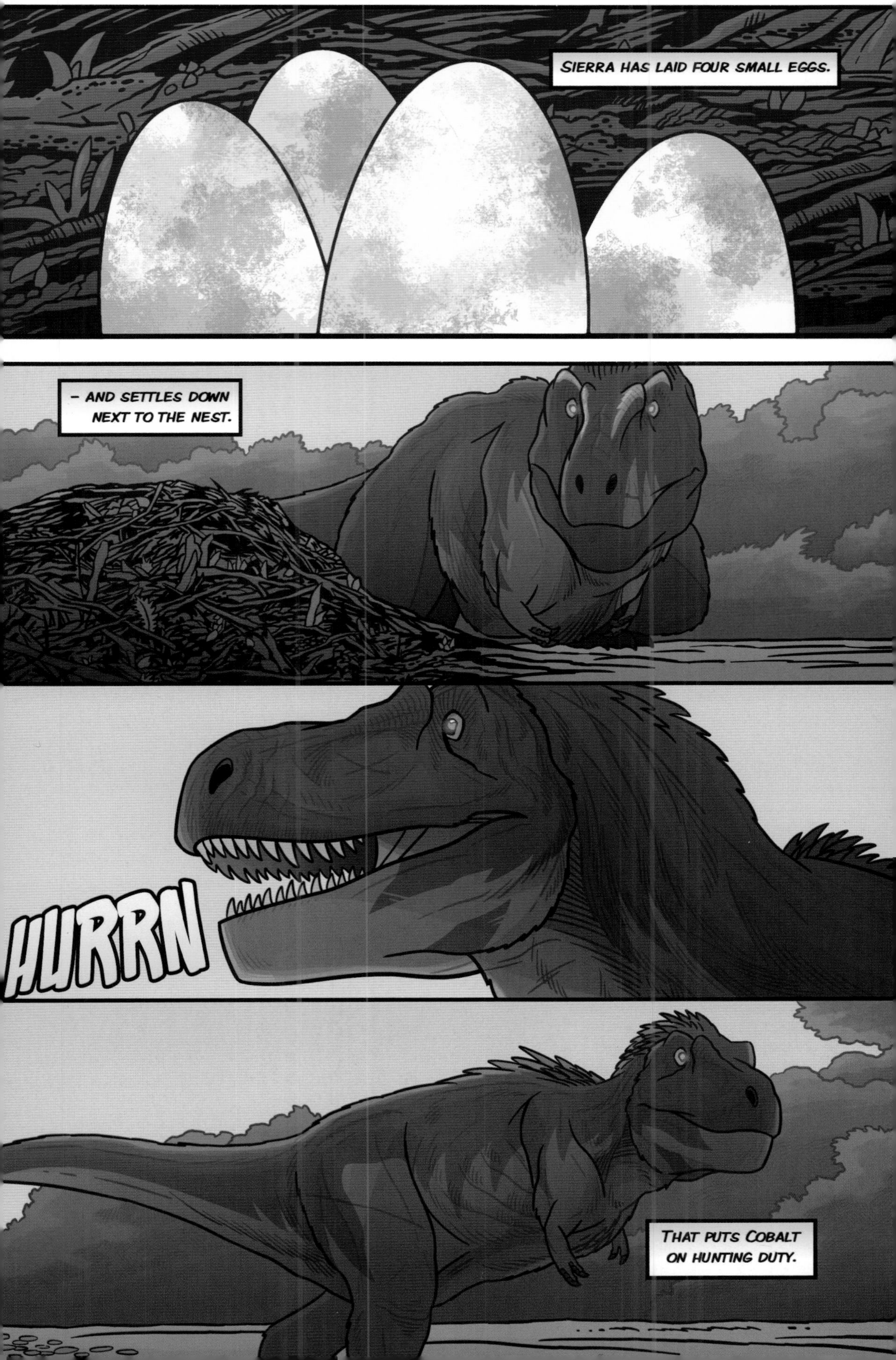
SIERRA HAS LAID FOUR SMALL EGGS.
– AND SETTLES DOWN NEXT TO THE NEST.
HURRN
THAT PUTS COBALT ON HUNTING DUTY.

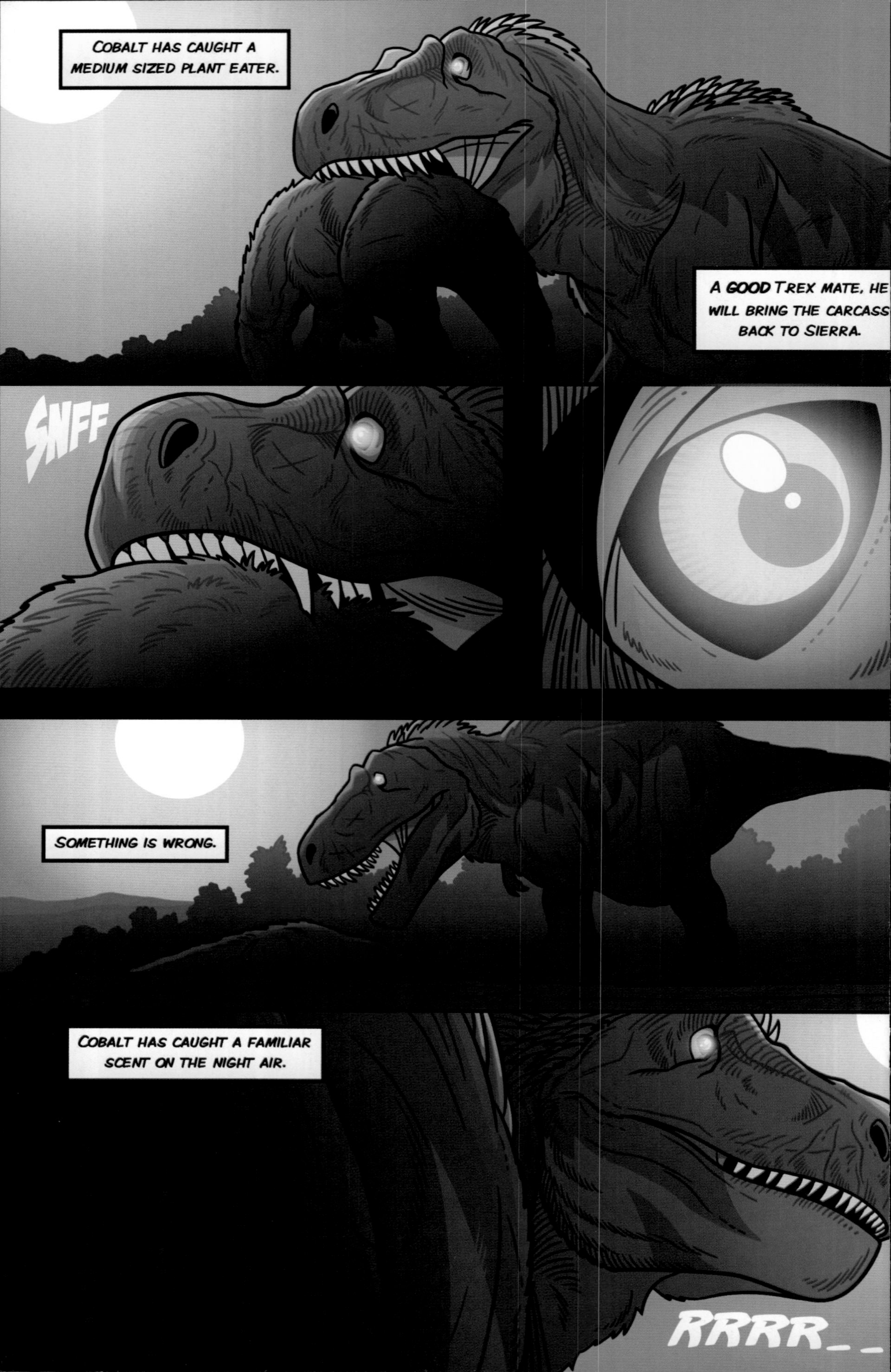
COBALT HAS CAUGHT A MEDIUM SIZED PLANT EATER.
A GOOD T.REX MATE, HE WILL BRING THE CARCASS BACK TO SIERRA.
SNFF
SOMETHING IS WRONG.
COBALT HAS CAUGHT A FAMILIAR SCENT ON THE NIGHT AIR.
RRRR_ _

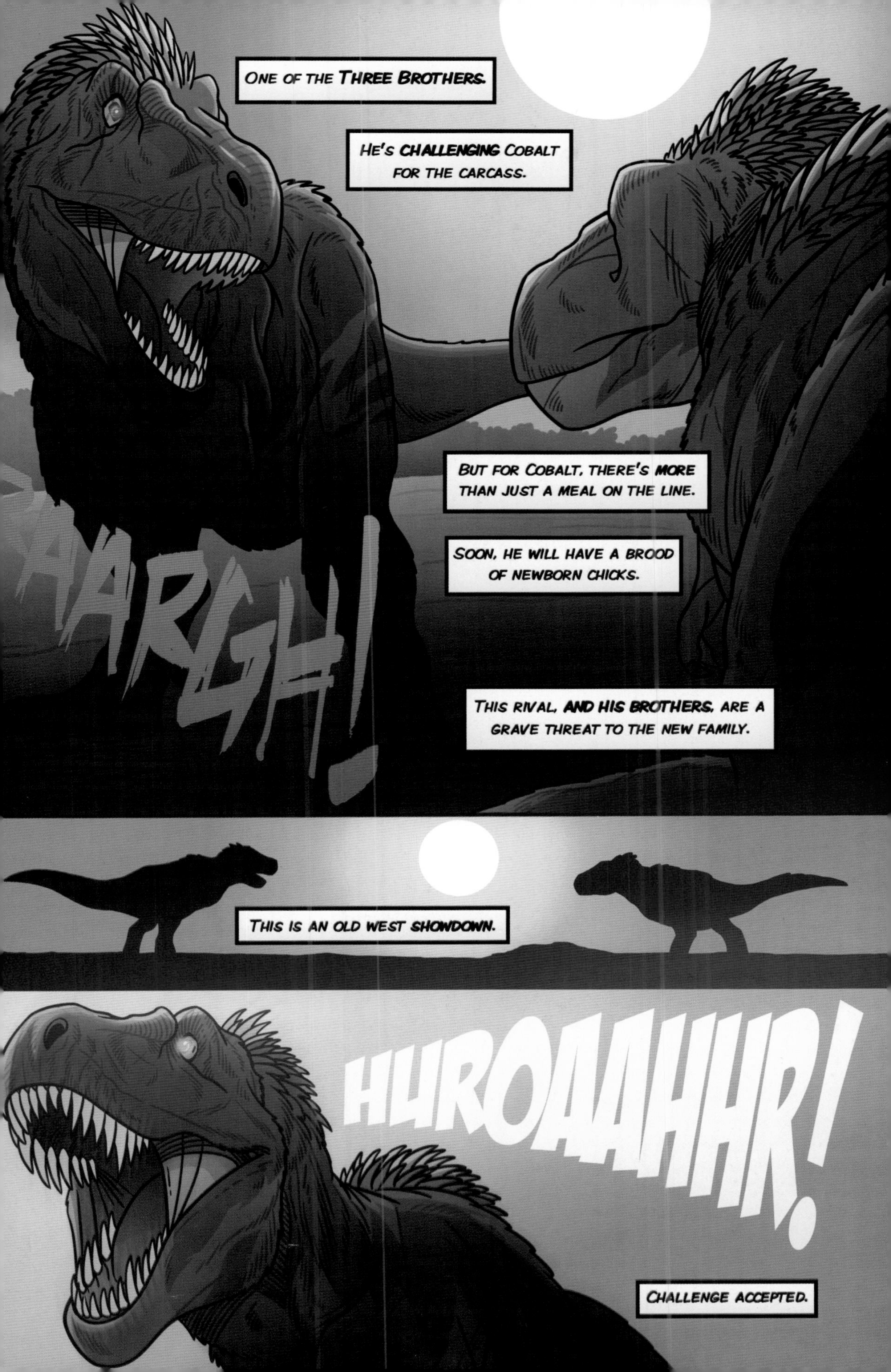
ONE OF THE THREE BROTHERS.
HE'S CHALLENGING COBALT FOR THE CARCASS.
AARGH!
BUT FOR COBALT, THERE'S MORE THAN JUST A MEAL ON THE LINE.
SOON, HE WILL HAVE A BROOD OF NEWBORN CHICKS.
THIS RIVAL, AND HIS BROTHERS, ARE A GRAVE THREAT TO THE NEW FAMILY.
THIS IS AN OLD WEST SHOWDOWN.
HUROAAHHR!
CHALLENGE ACCEPTED.

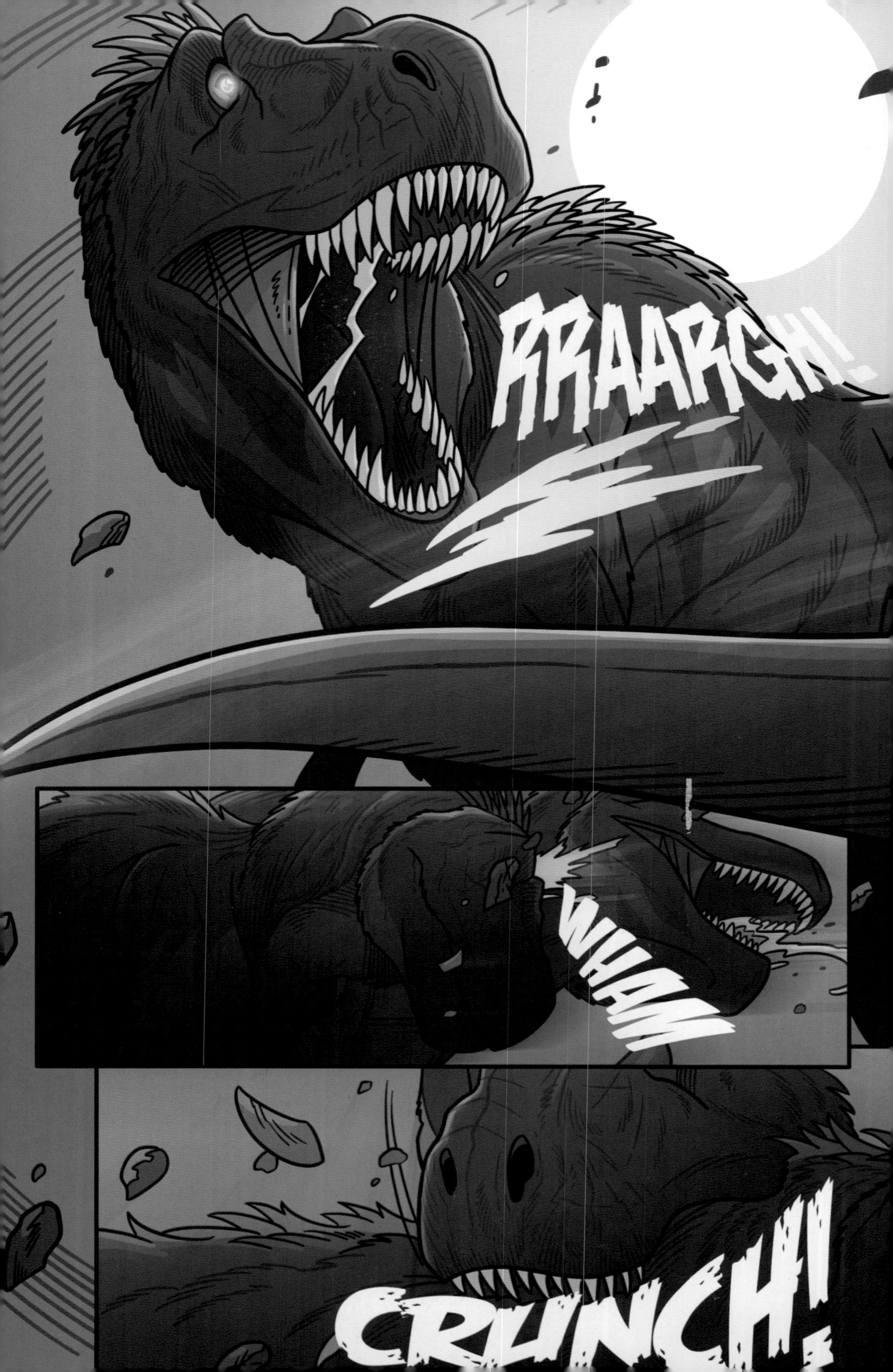
RRAARGH!
WHAM
CRUNCH!

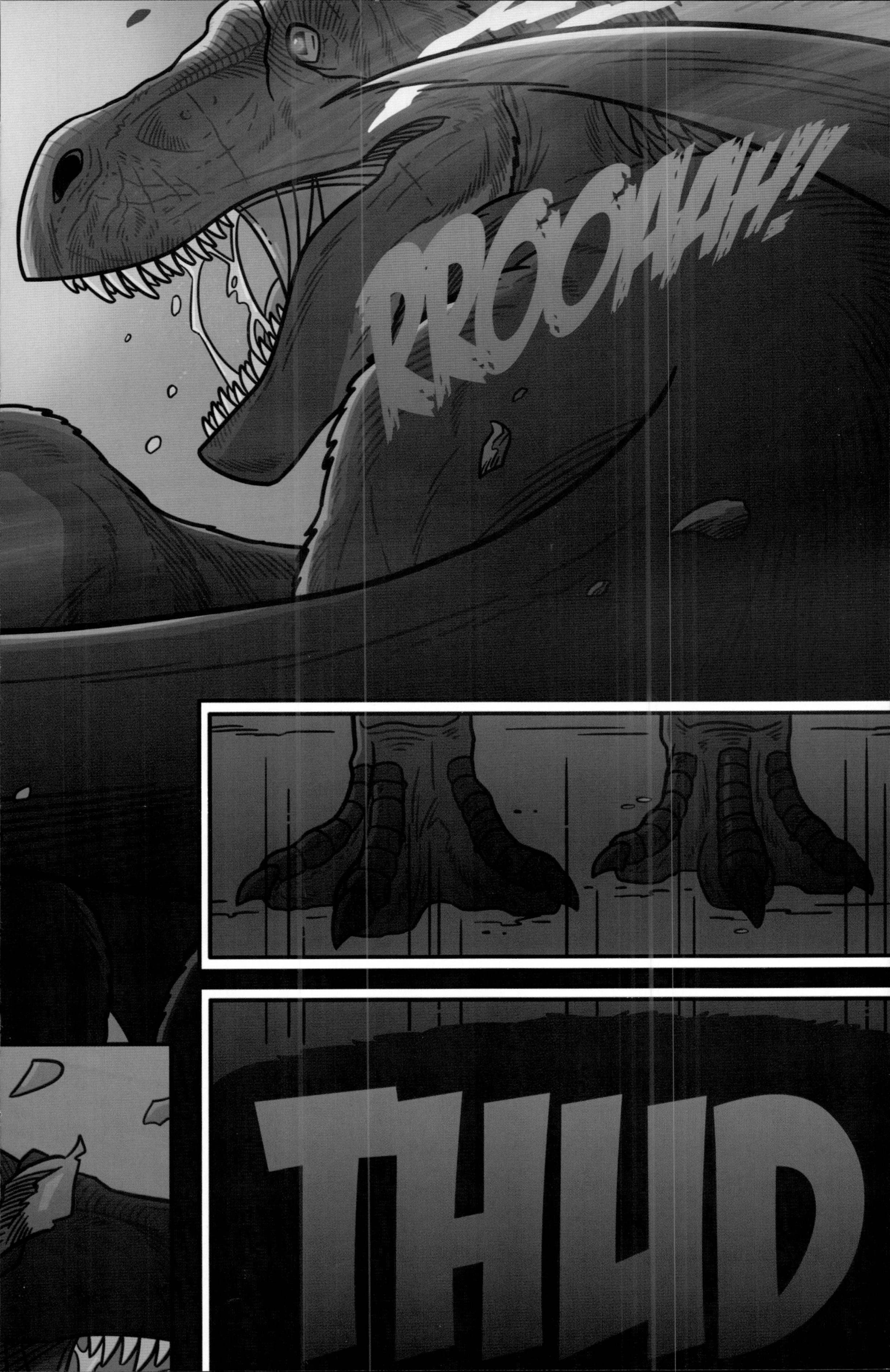
RROOAAHH!!
THUD

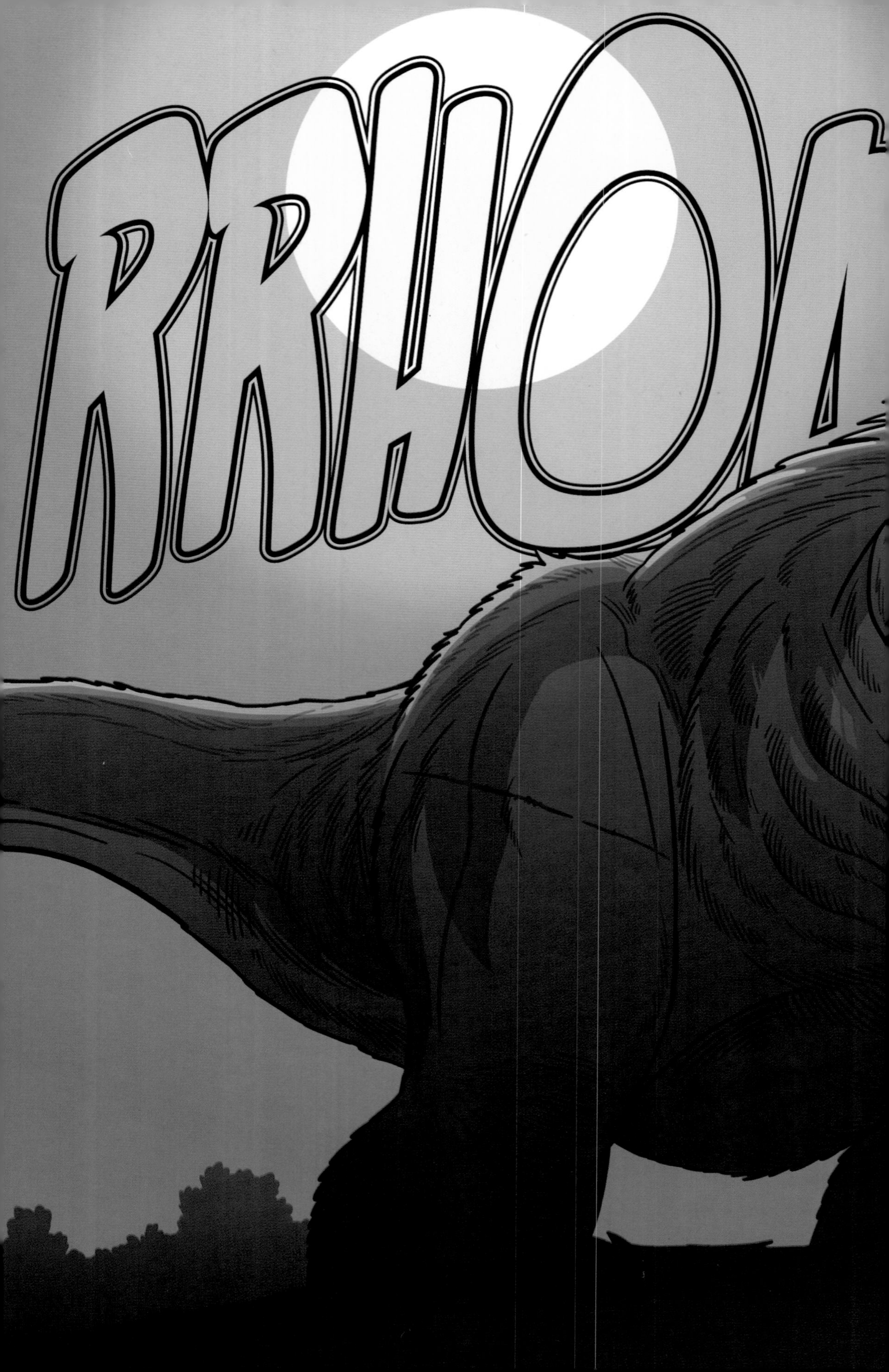
RRHOA

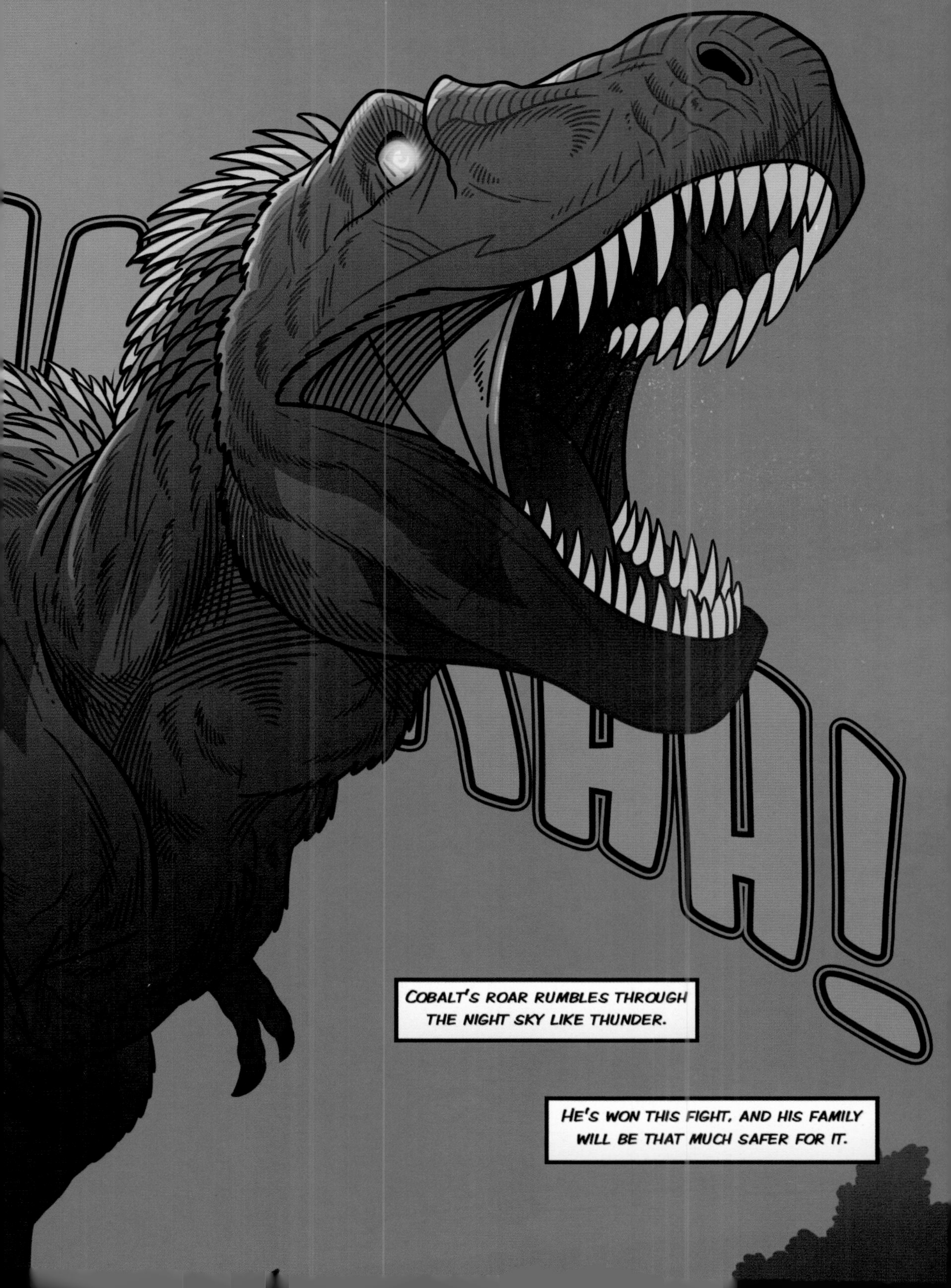
Cobalt's roar rumbles through the night sky like thunder.
He's won this fight, and his family will be that much safer for it.

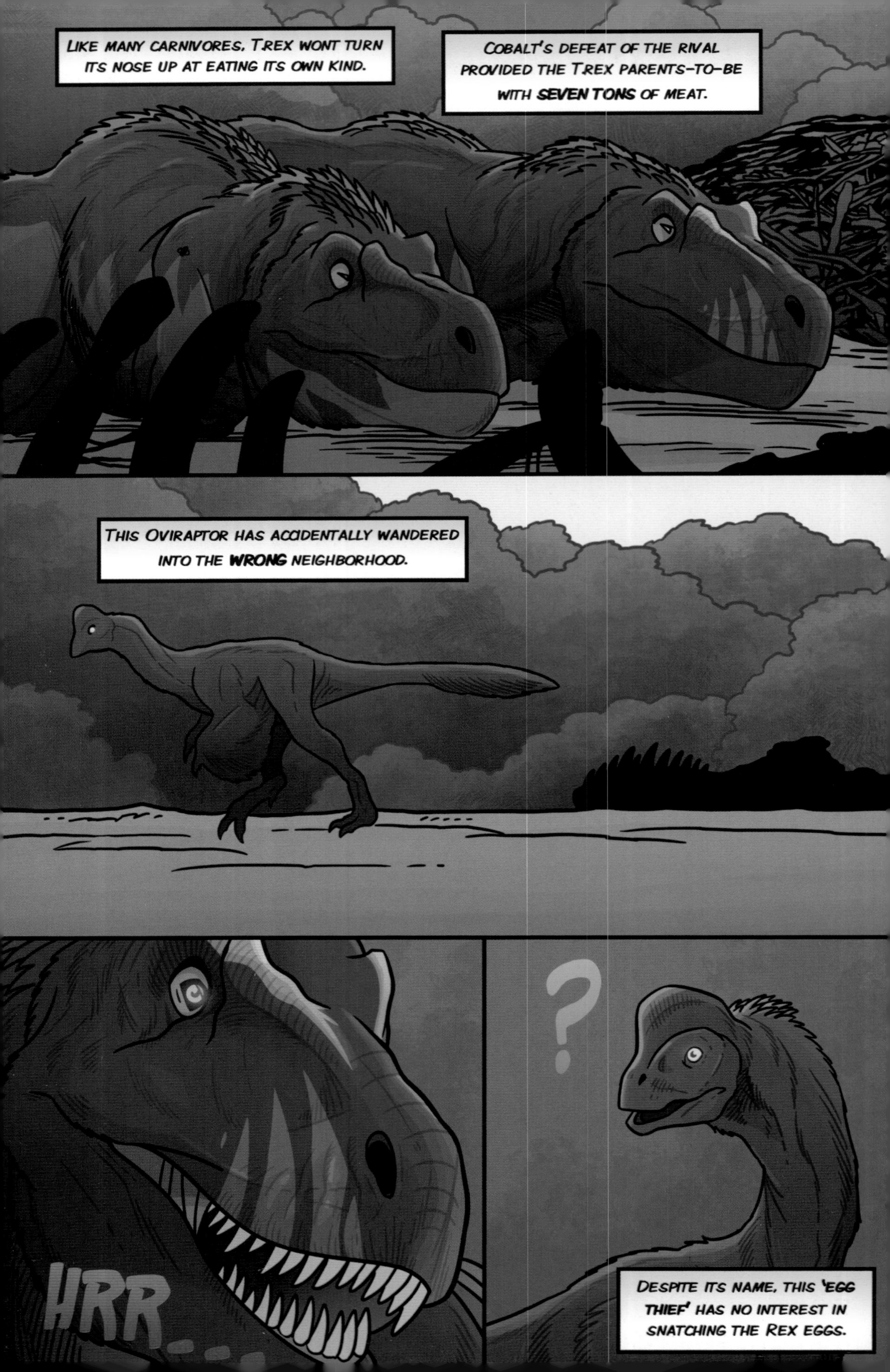
LIKE MANY CARNIVORES, T.REX WONT TURN ITS NOSE UP AT EATING ITS OWN KIND.
COBALT'S DEFEAT OF THE RIVAL PROVIDED THE T.REX PARENTS-TO-BE WITH SEVEN TONS OF MEAT.
THIS OVIRAPTOR HAS ACCIDENTALLY WANDERED INTO THE WRONG NEIGHBORHOOD.
HRR...
?
DESPITE ITS NAME, THIS 'EGG THIEF' HAS NO INTEREST IN SNATCHING THE REX EGGS.

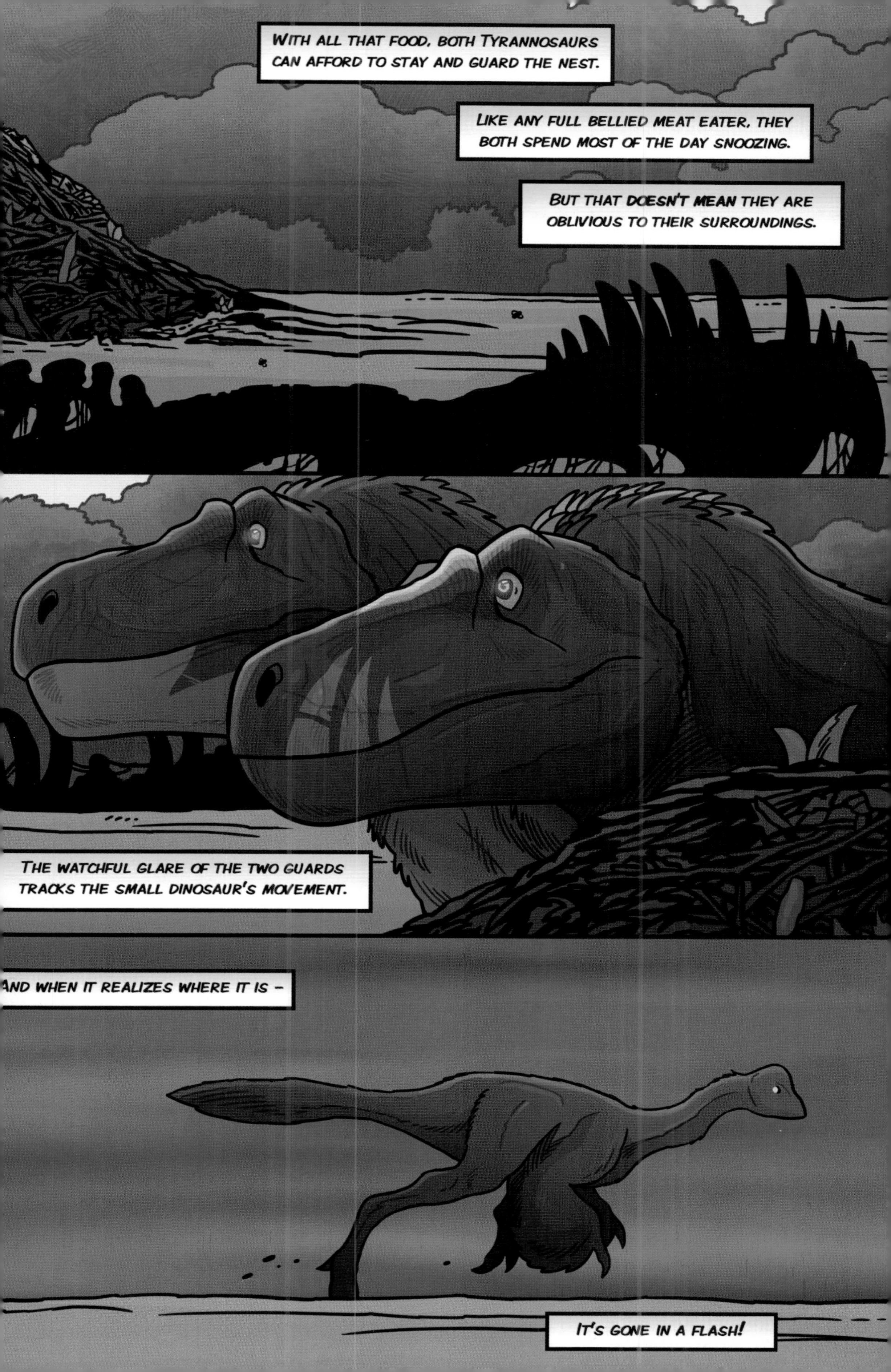
WITH ALL THAT FOOD, BOTH TYRANNOSAURS CAN AFFORD TO STAY AND GUARD THE NEST.
LIKE ANY FULL BELLIED MEAT EATER, THEY BOTH SPEND MOST OF THE DAY SNOOZING.
BUT THAT DOESN'T MEAN THEY ARE OBLIVIOUS TO THEIR SURROUNDINGS.
THE WATCHFUL GLARE OF THE TWO GUARDS TRACKS THE SMALL DINOSAUR'S MOVEMENT.
AND WHEN IT REALIZES WHERE IT IS –
IT'S GONE IN A FLASH!

UNDER COVER OF DARKNESS, COBALT QUIETLY DIGS INTO THE NEST.

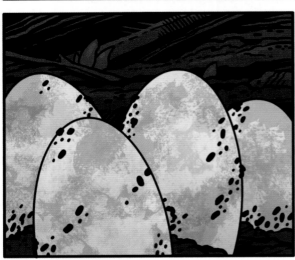

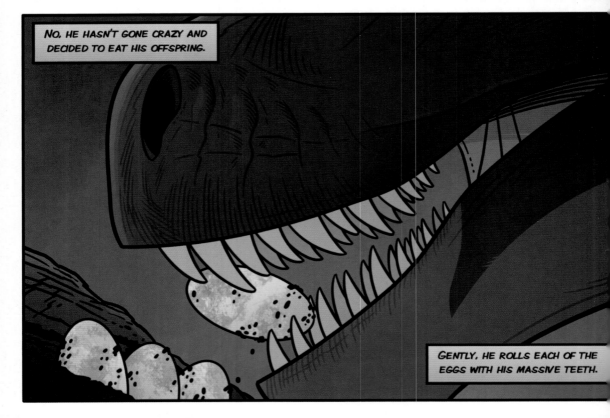

NO, HE HASN'T GONE CRAZY AND DECIDED TO EAT HIS OFFSPRING.

GENTLY, HE ROLLS EACH OF THE EGGS WITH HIS MASSIVE TEETH.

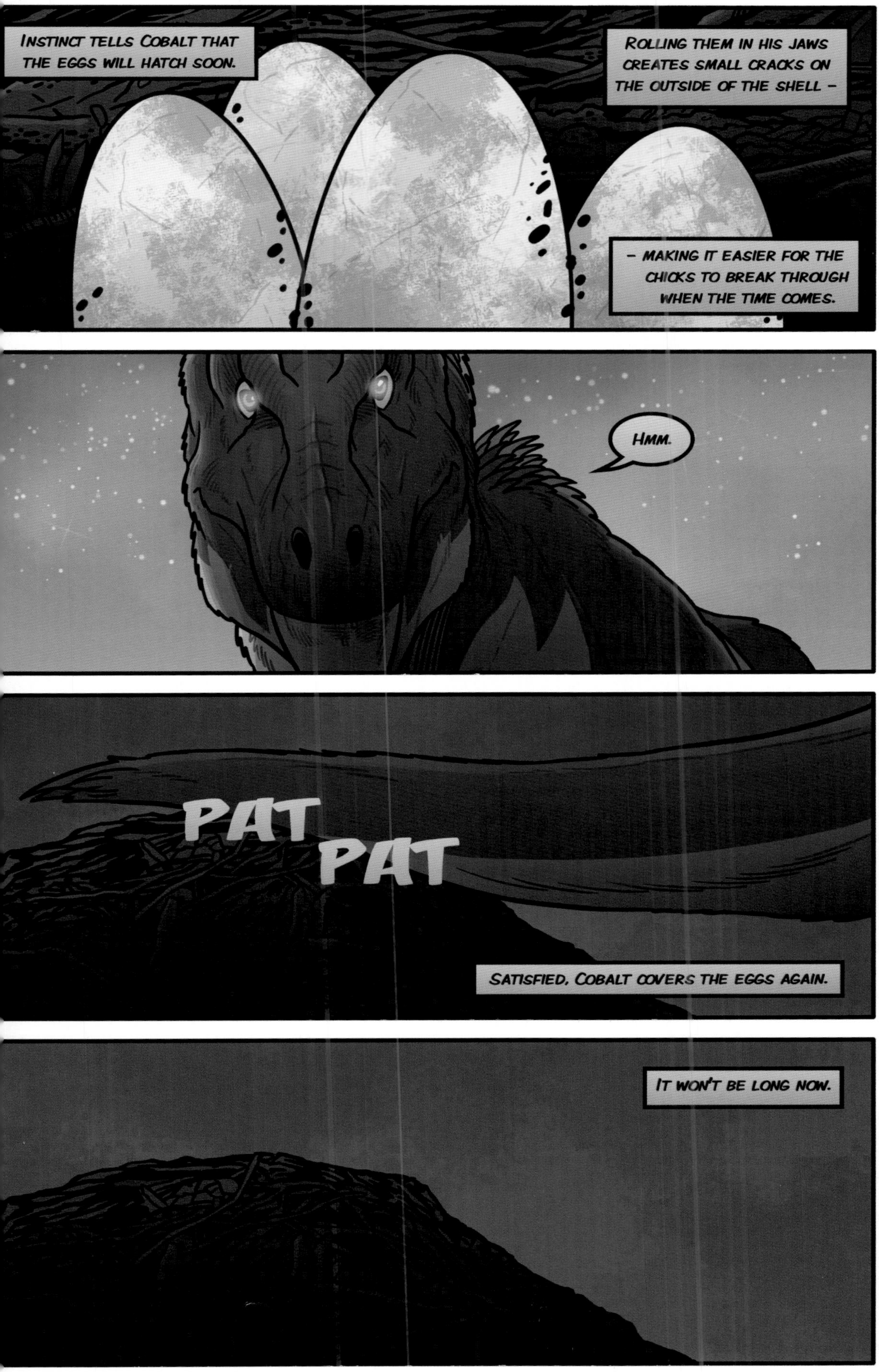
INSTINCT TELLS COBALT THAT THE EGGS WILL HATCH SOON.
ROLLING THEM IN HIS JAWS CREATES SMALL CRACKS ON THE OUTSIDE OF THE SHELL –
– MAKING IT EASIER FOR THE CHICKS TO BREAK THROUGH WHEN THE TIME COMES.
HMM.
PAT
PAT
SATISFIED, COBALT COVERS THE EGGS AGAIN.
IT WON'T BE LONG NOW.

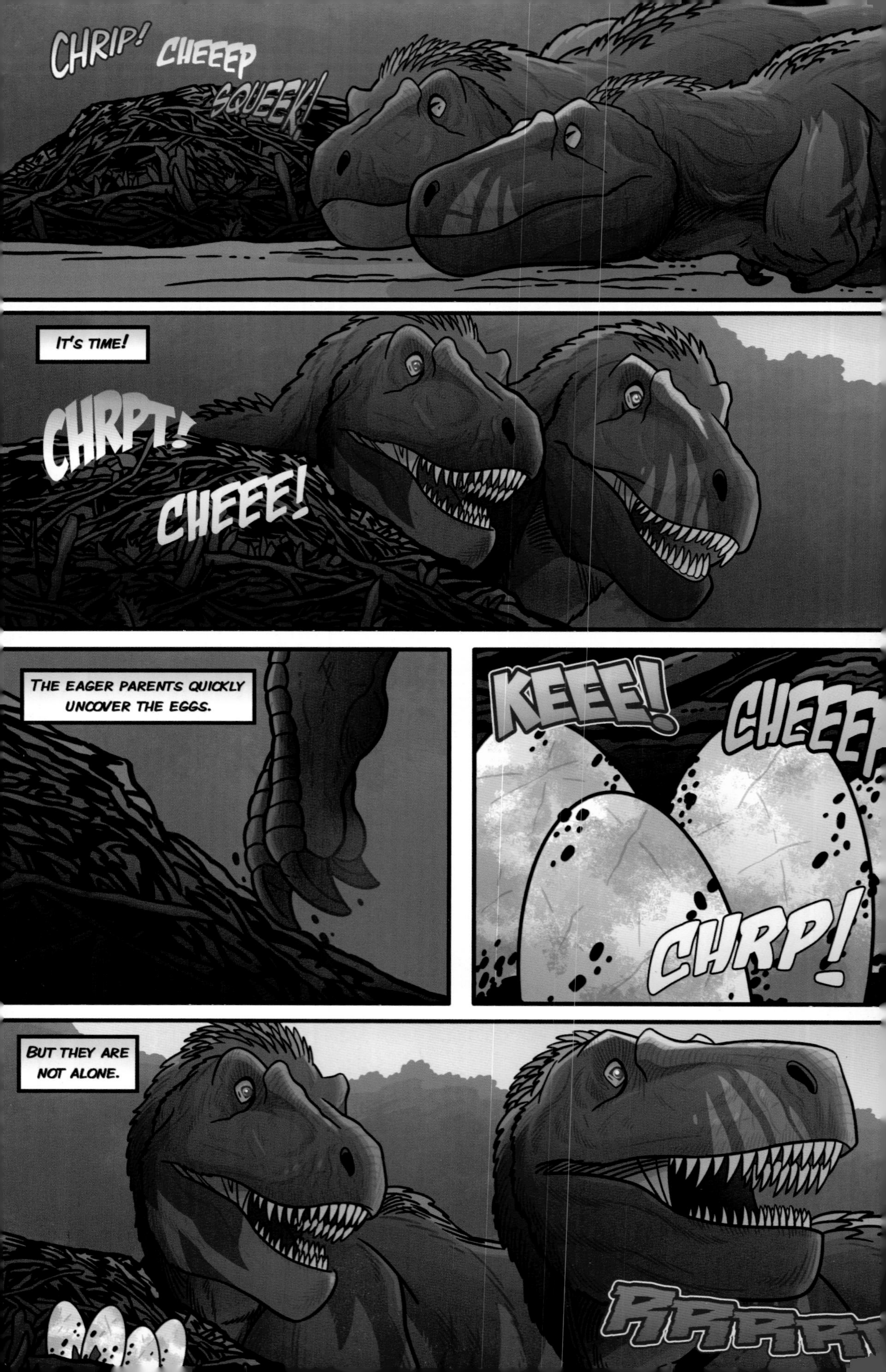
CHRIP! CHEEEP
SQUEEK!
IT'S TIME!
CHRPT!
CHEEE!
THE EAGER PARENTS QUICKLY UNCOVER THE EGGS.
KEEE!
CHEEEP
CHRP!
BUT THEY ARE NOT ALONE.
RRRRR

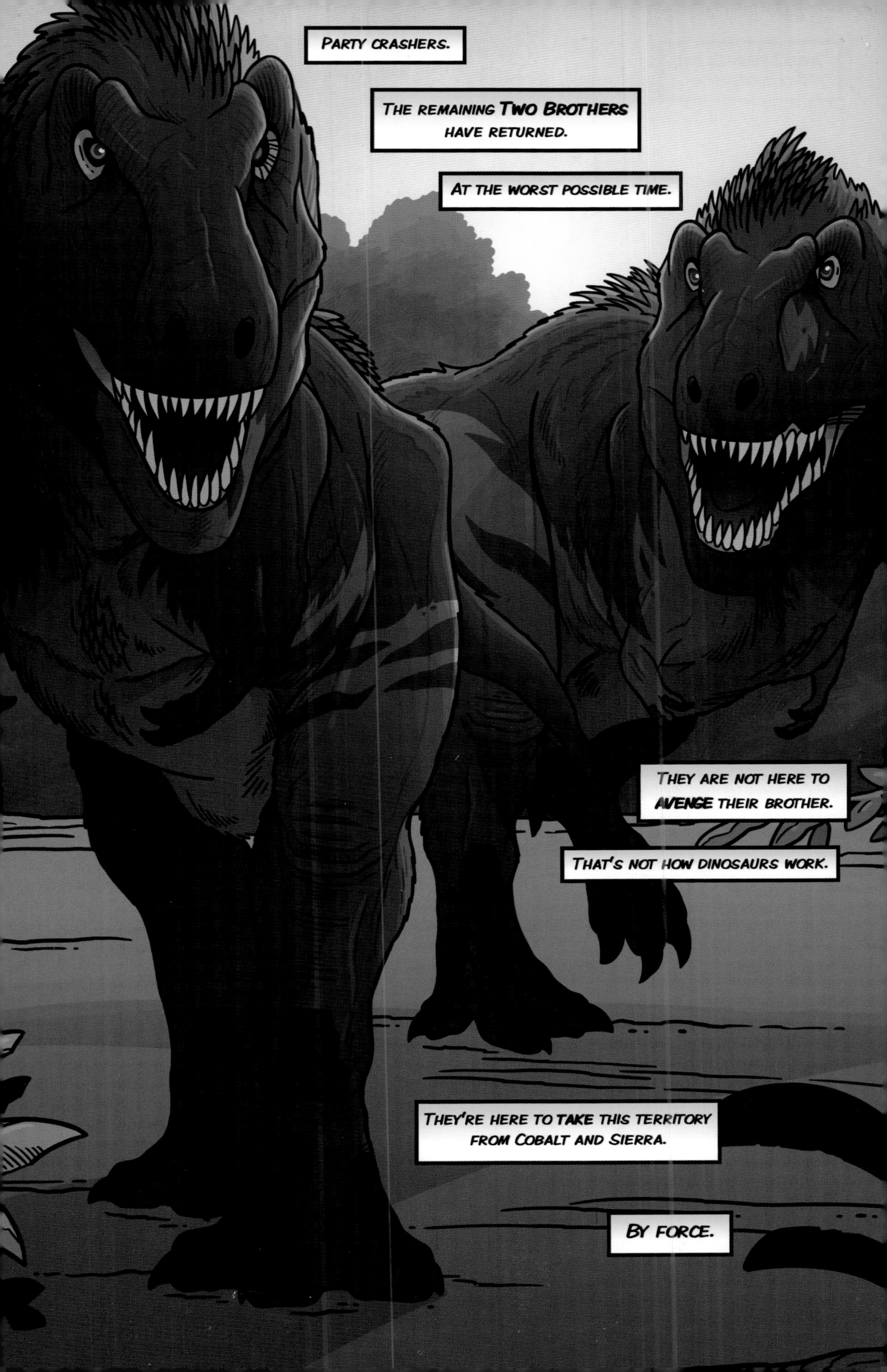
Party crashers.
The remaining Two Brothers have returned.
At the worst possible time.
They are not here to avenge their brother.
That's not how dinosaurs work.
They're here to take this territory from Cobalt and Sierra.
By force.

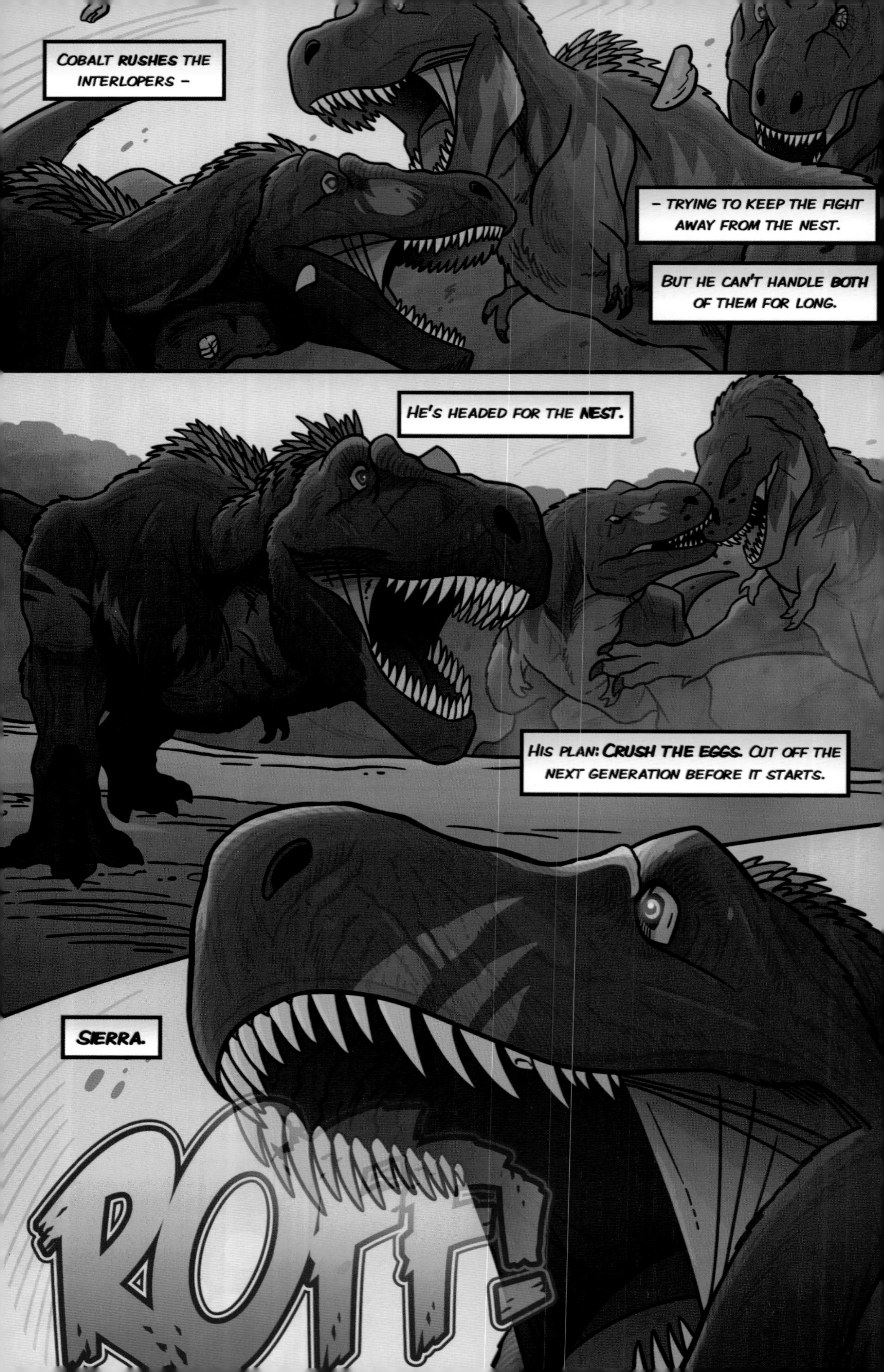
COBALT RUSHES THE INTERLOPERS –
– TRYING TO KEEP THE FIGHT AWAY FROM THE NEST.
BUT HE CAN'T HANDLE BOTH OF THEM FOR LONG.
HE'S HEADED FOR THE NEST.
HIS PLAN: CRUSH THE EGGS. CUT OFF THE NEXT GENERATION BEFORE IT STARTS.
SIERRA.
BOFF!

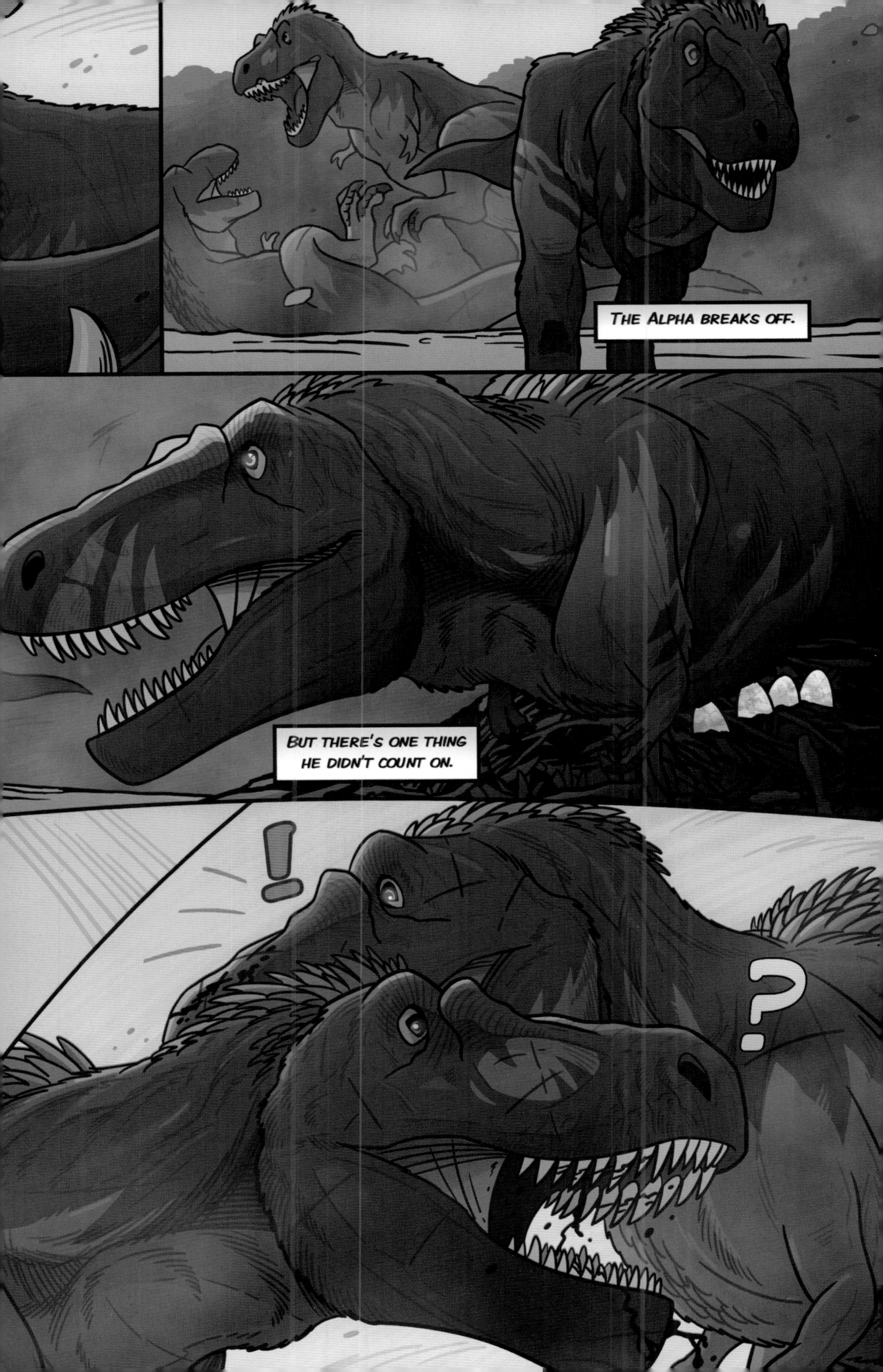

THE ALPHA BREAKS OFF.
BUT THERE'S ONE THING HE DIDN'T COUNT ON.
!
?

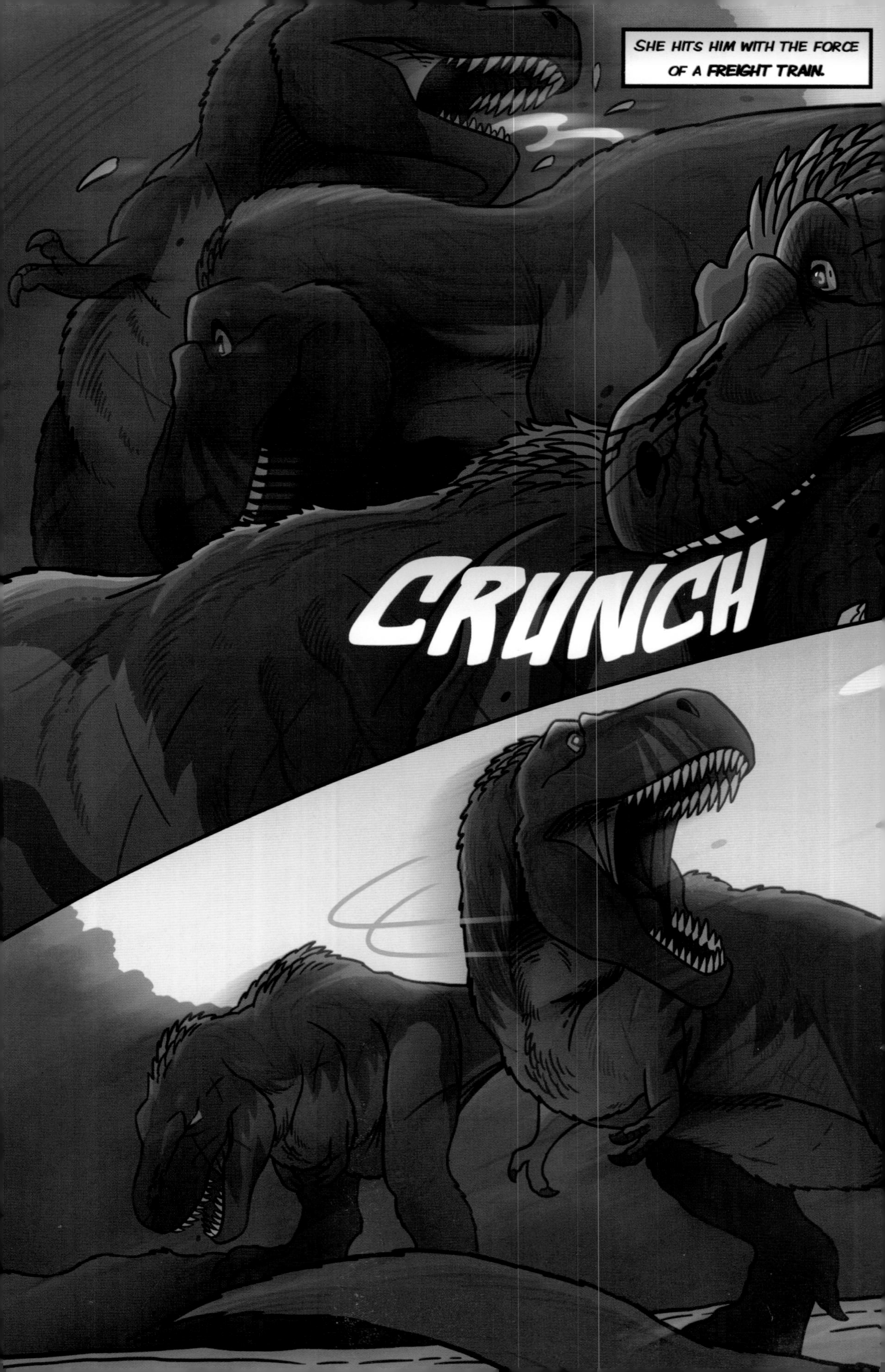
SHE HITS HIM WITH THE FORCE OF A FREIGHT TRAIN.
CRUNCH

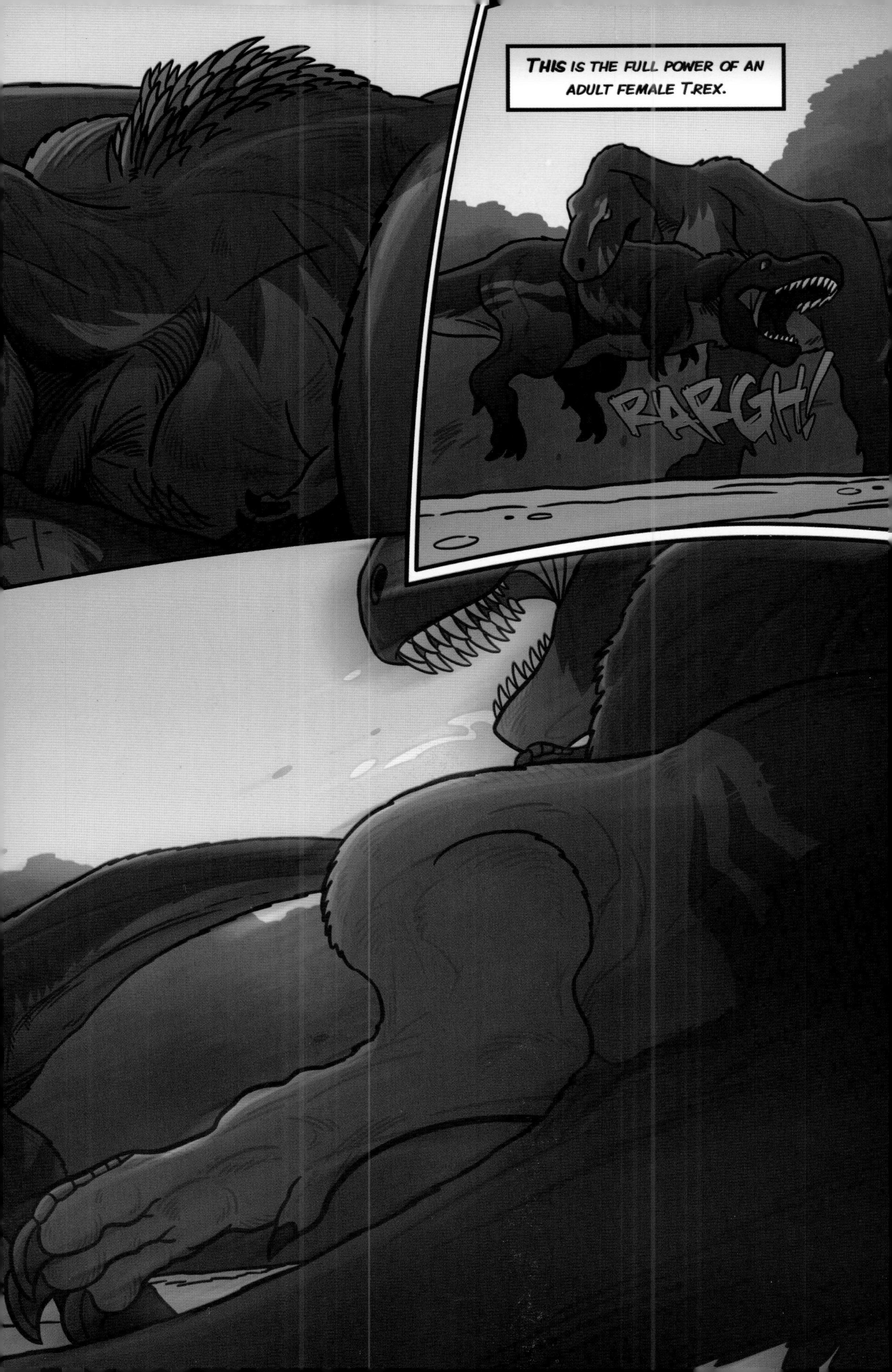
THIS IS THE FULL POWER OF AN ADULT FEMALE T.REX.
RARGH!

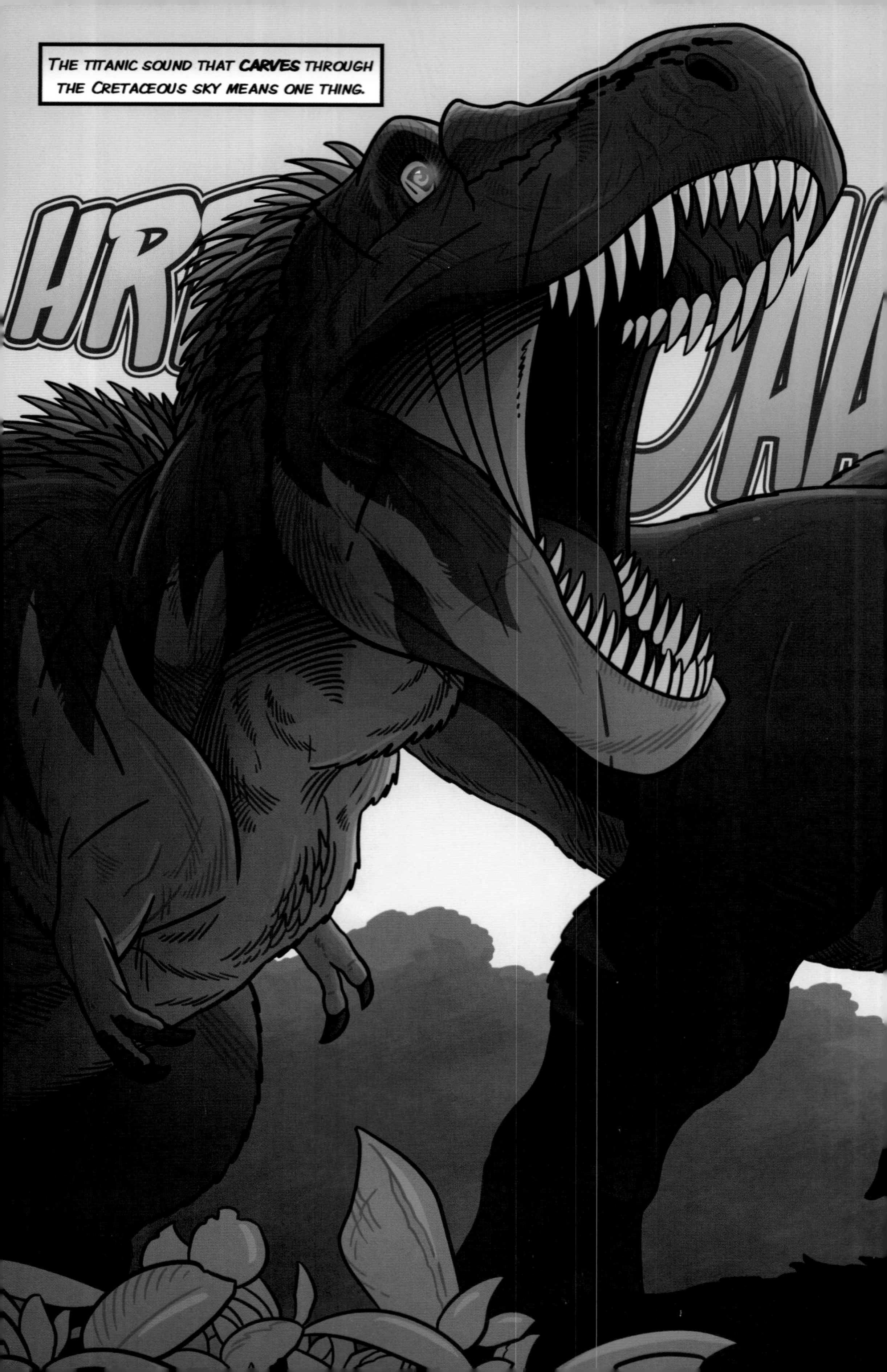
THE TITANIC SOUND THAT CARVES THROUGH THE CRETACEOUS SKY MEANS ONE THING.

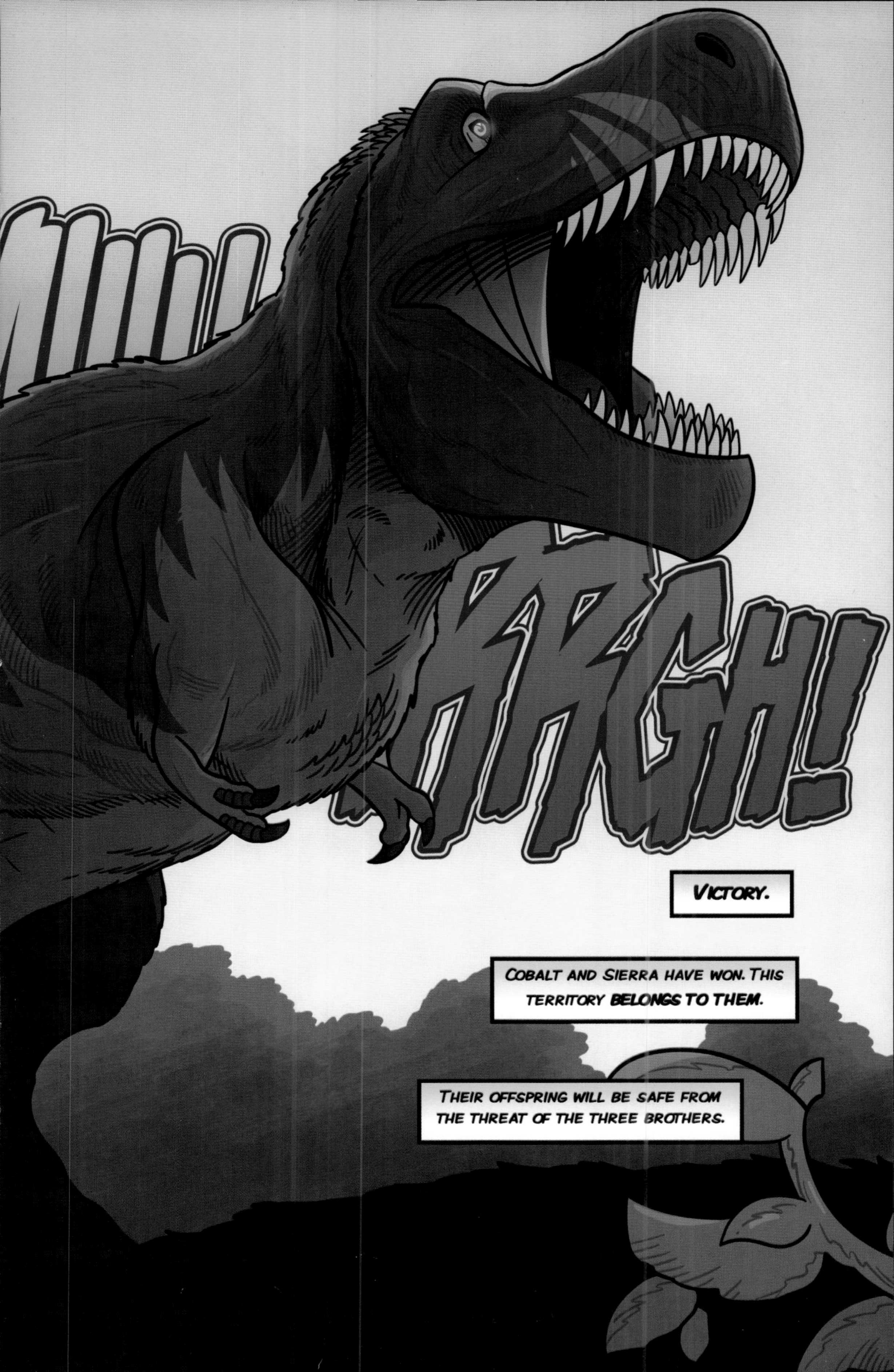
VICTORY.
COBALT AND SIERRA HAVE WON. THIS TERRITORY BELONGS TO THEM.
THEIR OFFSPRING WILL BE SAFE FROM THE THREAT OF THE THREE BROTHERS.

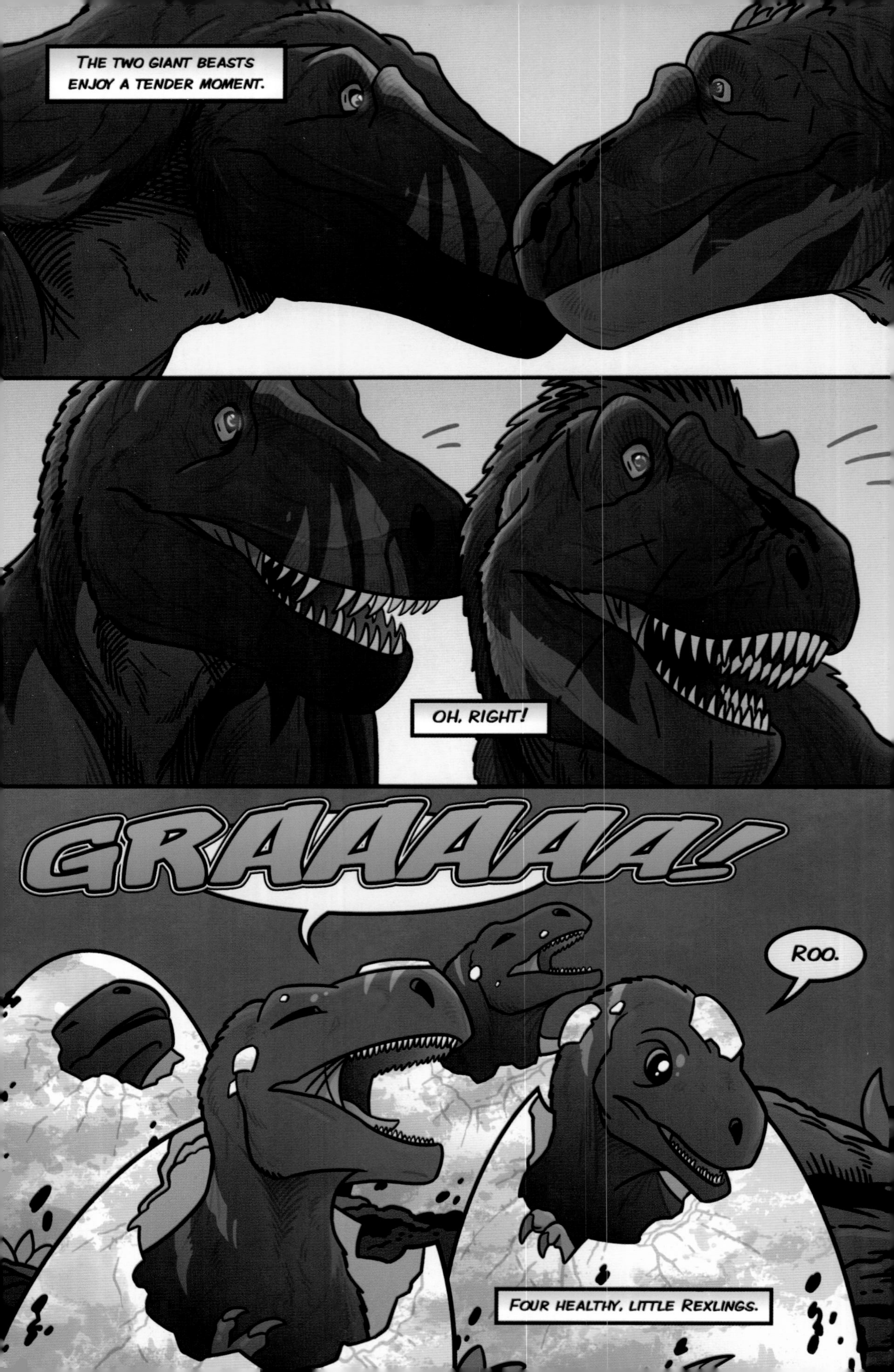
THE TWO GIANT BEASTS ENJOY A TENDER MOMENT.
OH, RIGHT!
GRAAAAAA!
ROO.
FOUR HEALTHY, LITTLE REXLINGS.

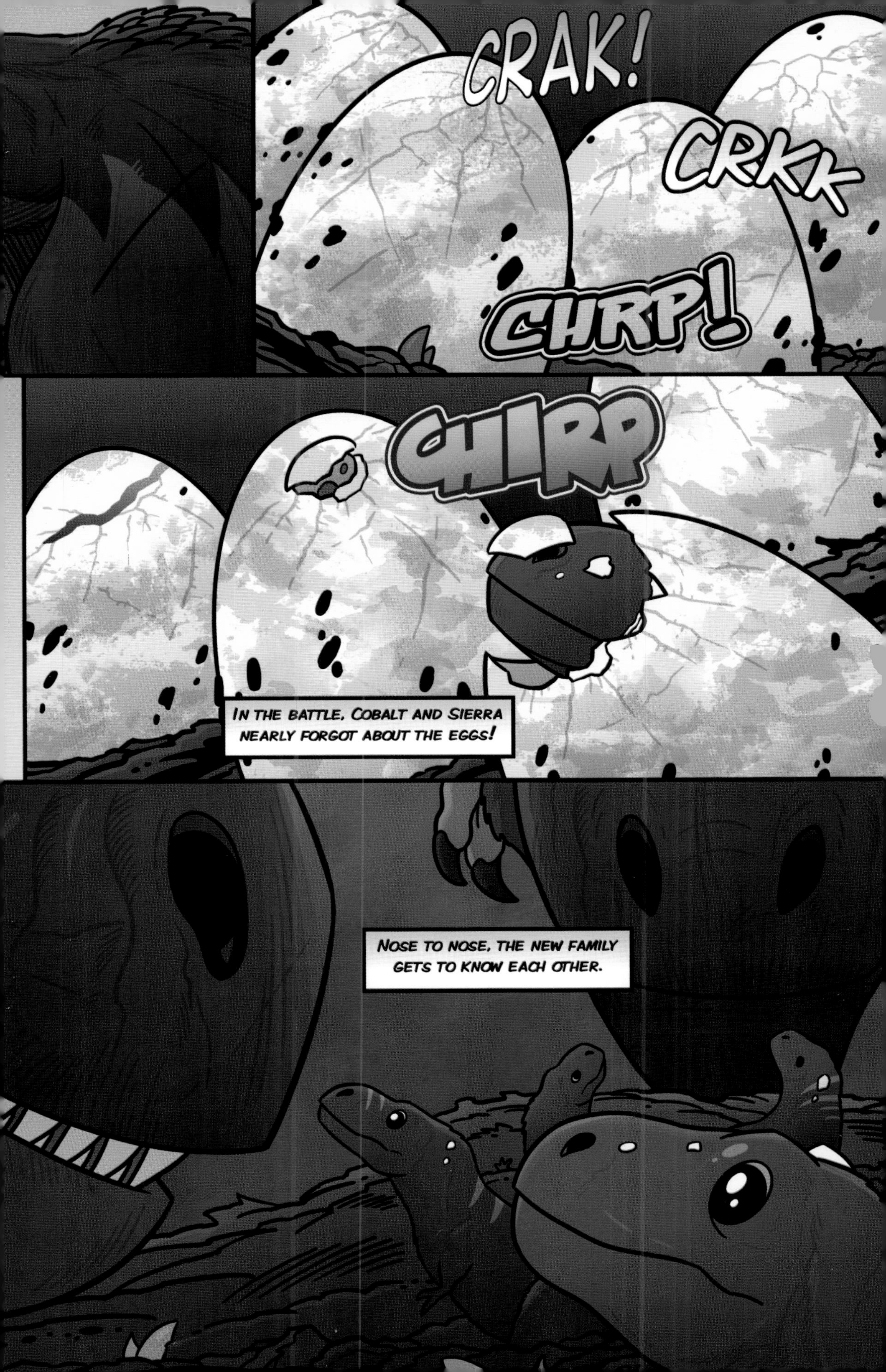
CRAK!
CRKK
CHRP!
CHIRP
IN THE BATTLE, COBALT AND SIERRA NEARLY FORGOT ABOUT THE EGGS!
NOSE TO NOSE, THE NEW FAMILY GETS TO KNOW EACH OTHER.

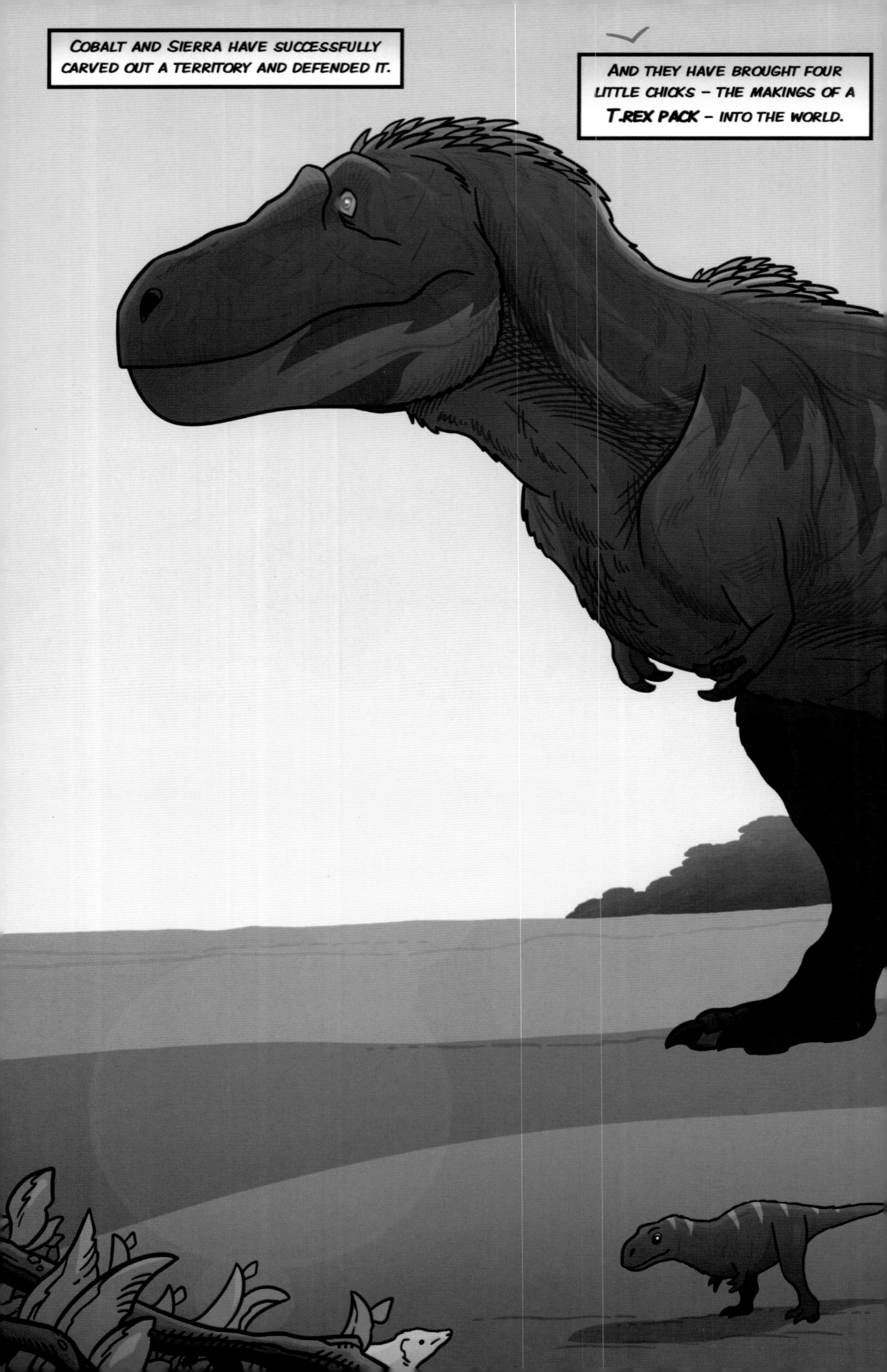
COBALT AND SIERRA HAVE SUCCESSFULLY CARVED OUT A TERRITORY AND DEFENDED IT.
AND THEY HAVE BROUGHT FOUR LITTLE CHICKS – THE MAKINGS OF A T.REX PACK – INTO THE WORLD.

LIFE WILL NOT BE EASY.
THIS IS STILL THE CRETACEOUS -
- A WORLD RULED BY TEETH.
BUT THESE ARE TYRANNOSAURUS REX -
- AND THEY HAVE THE BIGGEST TEETH.

TYRANNOSAURUS

REX

WRITTEN

&

ILLUSTRATED

BY

TED RECHLIN

PRESENTED

BY

REXTOOTH

STUDIOS

REXTOOTH
STUDIOS
REXTOOTH.COM